UTOPIA/DYSTOPIA?

UTOPIA/DYSTOPIA?

Edited by
PEYTON E. RICHTER
BOSTON UNIVERSITY

SCHENKMAN PUBLISHING COMPANY
CAMBRIDGE, MASSACHUSETTS

Schenkman books are distributed by
General Learning Press
250 James Street
Morristown, New Jersey

ISSUES IN CONTEMPORARY ETHICS
A Schenkman Series, Peter A. French, Editor

INDIVIDUAL AND COLLECTIVE RESPONSIBILITY:
The Massacre at My Lai
  Edited by Peter A. French

THE MANSON MURDERS:
A Philosophical Inquiry
  Edited by David E. Cooper

PUNISHMENT AND HUMAN RIGHTS
  Edited by Milton Goldinger

UTOPIA/DYSTOPIA?
  Edited by Peyton Richter

ASSASSINATION
  Edited by Harold Zellner

ABORTION
  Edited by Robert L. Perkins

Copyright © 1975

Schenkman Publishing Company
Cambridge, Massachusetts 02138

Library of Congress Catalog Card Number: 73-82378
Printed in the United States of America

ISBN 0-87073-537-3

CONTENTS

Preface   vii

PEYTON E. RICHTER

Utopia/Dystopia?: Threats of Hell or Hopes of Paradise   I

JOSEPH H. WELLBANK

Utopia and the Constraints of Justice   29

PRESTON N. WILLIAMS

Black Perspectives on Utopia   43

WALTER L. FOGG

Technology and Dystopia   57

PAVEL KOVALY

Marxism and Utopia   75

MELVIN M. SCHUSTER

Skinner and the Morality of Melioration   93

WALTER H. CLARK

Drugs and Utopia/Dystopia   109

DORIS AND HOWARD HUNTER

Siddhartha* and A Clockwork Orange: Two Images of
Man in Contemporary Literature and Cinema   125

BIBLIOGRAPHY   143

To

F. Ashton Richter

and

Anna Forbes Liddell

PREFACE

This, the fourth volume of Issues in Contemporary Ethics, differs from the first three in that it does not examine a classic moral issue as exemplified by a particular contemporary event. Instead, this book features contributions by philosophers, humanists and theologians on the general topic of Utopia. There is considerable interest these days in alternative social engineering plans for our increasing urban populations, but it is by no means a recent preoccupation. The dream of a utopian society which would maximize resources and minimize waste is as old as mankind. The Hindu Varnas, Ashramas and Purusarthas offer visions of the perfect society. Plato's *Republic*, More's *Utopia* and countless other works constitute the Western tradition of Utopian thinking. In counterpoint to utopian thinking are major dystopian novels such as *1984* and *Brave New World* and the anti-utopian attacks of such renowned philosophers as Karl Popper.

This volume is not a re-examination of the great utopian schemes of the past. Professor Richter has assembled an important collection of new essays on utopian thinking in our society. Some of the authors offer utopian designs; others attack the very foundations of any utopian scheme. Still others analyze some recent examples of utopian/dystopian theory in contemporary literature and film.

Why should such a topic be included in a series of books on ethics? Ethics has always dealt with a man's relations with his fellow men. The structure of society dictates, in large measure, the kinds of interactions men have with each other. Plato knew this, as did Aristotle; but too frequently in modern ethical thinking the social structure has been divorced from moral considerations. We live in a technical age. It is the age of the engineer, as well as the age of the environmentalist. Often the two are at odds, and the result may be social, ecological and moral chaos. We are a population of urban animals, despite the pastoral leanings of some of the young. Ethically and ecologically we must learn to deal with ourselves as a social unit. Utopian thinking has always attempted to meet that need, and dystopian literature has always provided the necessary critical element, reminding social engineers of the dangers of too much technology and too little "humanology."

The essays in this volume are offered in the hope that they will help generate serious ethical thinking on the part of philosophy students concerned with their future society. Some of the views taken by the authors may sound drastic. The views of the contributors are their own. There is no attempt by Professor Richter to suggest that any one theory is more worthy than any other. It is left to the reader to deal with the ultimate social question: Utopia/Dystopia?

—Peter A. French, Ph. D.
University of Minnesota, Morris

Utopia/Dystopia? : Threats of Hell or
Hopes of Paradise?
PEYTON E. RICHTER

"Oh, threats of Hell and Hopes of Paradise!
One thing at least is certain—This Life
  flies,
    One thing is certain and the rest is Lies;
The Flower that once has blown for ever
  dies."

Rubaiyat of Omar Khayyam
translated by Edward FitzGerald

THINKING UTOPIAN

"AN ACRE IN MIDDLESEX is better than a principality in Utopia," wrote Thomas Babington Macaulay, expressing in a sentence the so-called practical attitude toward a way of thinking that has aroused the enthusiasm of theorists from Plato to B. F. Skinner and evoked the wit of satirists from Aristophanes to Aldous Huxley. Utopian thinking, its defenders have assured us, is of supreme value in helping men and women to envisage an ideal social order by means of which to evaluate and to reform both states of affairs and affairs of state. Without this kind of imaginative speculation which proceeds to the very limits of rational possibility and tries valiantly to transcend them, human beings might long ago have grown content with their lot and failed to look beyond the immediate to the ultimate gratification. "The Utopians wonder," wrote Sir Thomas More in the first so-named *Utopia* (1516), "how any man should be so much taken with the glaring doubtful lustre of a jewel or stone, that can look up to a

Peyton E. Richter is Professor of Humanities at Boston University College of Basic Studies and editor of *Utopias: Social Ideals and Communal Experiments.* Consult the Bibliography for works by authors mentioned in this essay.

3

star, or to the sun himself." Utopians continually wonder why
human beings can be so absorbed in the gross pursuit of material
things that they fail to take the time to reflect on the glorious
possibilities that lie everywhere around and within them. Why
settle for a world that is ugly, polluted, filled with suffering,
grief, and despair, that is, in a word, imperfect, if we can envisage and through our efforts grasp a world which is beautiful,
clean, and filled with satisfaction, joy and hope—a utopian
world which is, in a word, perfect? Such a world, or at least such
a city-state, is conceivable, as Plato argued over two thousand
years ago in his *Republic*, but only if philosopher-rulers can
be produced and placed in positions of supreme power in a
rationally-ordered state. Such a world is possible, argues the
utopian psychologist B. F. Skinner in *Walden Two* (1948) and in
his recent *Beyond Freedom and Dignity* (1971), but only if refined
techniques of behavioral engineering can be developed and ap-
plied as soon as possible to bring to an end the undesirable
behavior of a world running amuck.

Some defenders of utopian thinking, Lewis Mumford, for example, have valued it both as a harmless mode of escape for the
restless and dissatisfied and as an instrument of social reconstruction. Others, such as Arthur E. Morgan, have seen in
utopian literature an invaluable repository of "traditions of
innovation" and a source of inspiration, guidance, and influence. The great sociologist of knowledge, Karl Mannheim,
analyzed the relationship of utopia to ideology, and saw in
utopia a vision of the future which could inspire collective
action to change the social realities which are merely stabilized
and glossed over by ideology. Another sociologist, David Riesman, has defended utopian thinking as an antidote to over-
cautious thinking and uninspired reliance upon facts. Margaret Mead has shown how visions of utopias have been of vital
importance to people in different cultures in pursuing their way
of life and preserving their cultural identity. Finally, Alvin
Toffler, after stressing in *Future Shock* (1970) the importance
of utopian ideas in offering alternative futures for human fantasy and aspiration, calls for collaborative utopianism, "a
revolution in the production of utopias."

Whatever might be said or thought of utopian speculation,
a study of its historical development and various forms will

reveal it to be something which springs from deep within the human psyche, giving expression to the human need for rootedness as well as transcendence. Often what initially appears to be a genuinely novel idea in utopian thinking turns out in historical retrospect to have been long ago presented or at least presaged. For, as Glenn Negley points out in his essay in this volume, "The limitations and the repetitious impact of ordinary language tend to create the illusion that in the coinage and propagation of a new linguistic expression we have thereby discovered or created a new factual configuration." This does not mean that utopian speculation has no novelties—it is filled with dazzling surprises and brilliant leaps forward—it simply means that it has a history which makes its novelties obvious if not predictable.

DYSTOPIAN DEMURRERS

Critics of utopian thinking and planning have attacked both the methods and the goals of utopians. The ancient Greek philosopher Aristotle attacked his teacher Plato's ideal city-state, as described in *The Republic*, for sacrificing the values of individual self-fulfillment in order to achieve the values of group cohesion. Too much unity or identity of interests can lead to social defects, such as loss of individual identity, just as too little unity can lead to other defects, such as loss of corporate security and order. Also, collectivization of property, Aristotle warns, usually undermines individual interest in it and weakens motivation for caring for it. Where everything belongs to everybody, nobody will care about anything. Further, Aristotle attributes the cause of many social ills to "the wickedness of human nature" which, he thinks, is often overlooked by utopian planners in their enthusiasm for social panaceas. These considerations, however, did not prevent Aristotle from proffering his own utopian proposals in his *Politics*, but they did condition and define the limits within which he speculated.

In the present century Aldous Huxley in *Brave New World* (1932) also criticizes the goals of overall utopian planning insofar as they direct human efforts toward "community, identity and stability" at the expense of privacy, diversity, and change. Dystopia, not utopia, he fears, is emerging. Huxley's vision of

a technologically perfect world of the future in which everyone
has been made perfectly happy through scientific breeding,
conditioning, and drugs, is as much a vision of hell to him as
it is a viable and desirable vision of heaven on earth to some
current defenders of utopias.

When Huxley's hero John Savage defiantly asserts the values
of individual striving, suffering, and loving before the benevolent but autocratic world controller Mustapha Mond, he is
giving expression to a utopian tradition which the Frenchman
Jean Jacques Rousseau had given voice to in the eighteenth
century and the Russian Eugene Zamiatin had powerfully expressed in the early twentieth century in his satirical novel *We*
(1924). This dystopian work influenced not only Huxley's
Brave New World but also George Orwell's *1984*. In Zamiatin's
dystopia men have been dehumanized by absolute collectivization; freedom of thought, action and imagination have been
rigorously curtailed; and an authoritarian rational control has
been imposed upon every detail of everyone's life by the malevo-
lent "Well-Doer." "Reason prevails" before and after a brief
and unsuccessful attempt at rebellion led by the book's nameless (but not numberless) hero. Realizing how quickly the ardor
of revolution had cooled and petrified, Zamiatin wrote *We* both
as a protest against the destruction of freedom and individuality by rational but heartless fanatics, and as an appeal for continuous, self-critical revolutionary consciousness, without the
revitalizing influence of which, he believed, imagination and
feeling would atrophy, leaving a cruel barren reason in control
of a joyless paradise.

With less subtlety and more bitter irony than Zamiatin, George
Orwell attacked collectivistic utopias first in *Animal Farm*
(1946) and later in *1984* (1949). The society depicted in *1984*
is one in which absolute power has been allowed to corrupt
so absolutely that moral judgments are considered not merely
relative to individuals or groups, but self-contradictory and
nonsensical. Knowledge is defined as ignorance, love as hate,
freedom as slavery, war as peace. Thought-control has been
achieved by the manipulation of language. Privacy, pleasure,
and mystery have been taken out of sex and reproduction by the
interference of state authority. Science has become the hand-
maiden of a destructive technology, and the free spirit of

scientific inquiry has withered away. Big Brother, the symbol of the super-state's power, triumphs over all disloyal citizens such as Orwell's hero Winston Smith, who after a feeble period of nonconformity, is brainwashed into submission to the Party and doomed to a living death and (eventually) to a death devoid of all meaning.

In light of such dystopian visions of utopian planning one may be inclined, as was Huxley when he wrote *Brave New World*, to agree with the Russian philosopher Nikolas Berdyaev that the pressing problem of today is not how to reach utopia but how to avoid it. "It was wonderful to find America," Mark Twain has Pudd'nhead Wilson note under October 12 on his calendar, "but it would have been more wonderful to miss it."

The dychotomy between the utopian and the dystopian is misleading, however, if one thinks "once a utopian or a dystopian, always a utopian or dystopian." A utopian can sometimes temporarily wear the mask of a dystopian and vice versa. Huxley donned the dystopian mask when he wrote one of the most influential modern dystopias, *Brave New World*, only to discard it later when he wrote his constructive utopia *Island* (1962). The most famous, influential and prolific of all writers of utopias, H. G. Wells, after writing scores of optimistic scenarios for the future, ended his life as an embittered dystopian, despairing of all hope for the human race, recording his bleakest misgivings in his final essay "A Mind at the End of its Tether." Karl Marx and Friedrich Engels in the *Communist Manifesto* (1848) condemned utopian schemes for social improvement and heralded the prospect of a communist revolution. Many years later, in *Socialism: Utopian and Scientific* (1892), Engels contrasted what were to him the naive, unrealistic and impractical programs of social reconstruction of Cabet, Fourier and others with what he claimed was the only truly scientific socialism, the socialism based on his and Marx's dialectical materialism. Yet despite their disclaimers, as Pavel Kovaly makes clear in his essay in this volume, Engels and Marx were utopian thinkers. Their vision of a classless society, their proposals for bringing it about, the idealistic fervor with which they defended it, their inability to tolerate criticism of it—all are signs of a kind of utopian commitment rather than an impartial scientific open-mindedness.

Many other objections to concepts of utopia have been brought forward by dystopians. Thinkers as different as Feodor Dostoyevsky and Joseph Wood Krutch have objected to the kind of utopian thinker who tries to comprehend, predict and control human behavior on the basis of a materialistic and mechanistic philosophy of life. Human behavior, they argue, is far too complex, mysterious, and spontaneous to be encompassed by any materialism—mechanistic or dialectical. Despite the fact that in the course of history men have often been exploited and enslaved, caged and cajoled, and have sometimes denied and even tried to escape from freedom, man has remained essentially a free and spontaneous agent. When pushed too far man will thumb his nose at his would-be controllers and shatter their crystal palaces of perfection which would violate human autonomy and interfere with freely chosen life-styles. Man will always misbehave if only just to spite the behaviorists. The monkey in man will usually manage to throw a monekywrench into the machinery rather than allow himself to be dominated by it forever.

Other objections have focused on the means, the organization of human activities which would supposedly bring about utopias. The English nineteenth century philosopher and sociologist Herbert Spencer wrote some of the earliest and most vehement attacks on the idea of a regimented and collectivized society. The development of larger and larger bureaucracies, which by their very structure were authoritarian and self-perpetuating, foreshadowed, in Spencer's view, "the coming slavery" in which freedom of choice would be eliminated and every aspect of a person's life would be regulated by rule and decree. Following Spencer's lead, a later social critic, Friedrich Hayek, viewed the developments that were leading to the welfare state as "the road to serfdom." Aldous Huxley in *Brave New World Revisted* (1958) gave further warning of the dangers of over-organization and control of human activities by efficient but impersonal agencies oblivious to individual differences.

Contemporary writers have challenged utopian visions for still other reasons. Ralf Dahrendorf maintains that by stressing equilibrium and failing to take into account the facts of conflict and change, most utopian proposals distort the sociological field and mislead theoretical analysis. Karl Popper also objects that by demanding a finished, closed, completely planned society rather than an open, progressing, partially planned society, utopian builders can promote fanaticism and violence as their proponents impatiently press forward to achieve their pre-determined ends. In losing contact with immediate child-like perception, in failing to take into account cross-cultural materials, and in not relating expertise on the future to present and past knowledge, utopians lack vividness and persuasive-ness, says Margaret Mead. Finally, in Thomas Molnar's view—and this is one of the oldest objections to utopias—the claim that salvation can be achieved in history and that man can perfect his nature by his own efforts and remove all evils from his environment, is a kind of permanent heresy which leads man astray, diverting him from the true path to salvation through faith in the supernatural.

Utopia Rising

As the end of our century draws closer, there are innumerable signs of a resurgence of interest in utopian thinking and plan-ning. The first of these is a widespread interest in futurology, prognostication, and social speculation, exemplified by such works as Arthur C. Clarke's *Profiles of the Future* (1963) and Herman Kahn's and Anthony J. Wiener's *Toward the Year Two Thousand: A Framework for Speculation* (1967). Much of this speculation has centered on the present and future impact of science and technology. Walter Fogg, in his essay in this vol-ume, pays particular attention to this important area of utopian (and dystopian) thinking.

Closely related to futurology is the current interest in social and behavioral engineering, ranging from the optimistic, bril-liant and sometimes seemingly fantastic projects of R. Buck-minster Fuller (e.g. *Utopia or Oblivion*, 1969) to the more subtle and possibly more feasible proposals of B. F. Skinner *(Beyond Freedom and Dignity*, 1971). The implications of operant conditioning are presently being pondered; the advantages and disadvantages of behavioral control are being weighed; the techniques of the "new utopians," already active in the tech-netronic age, are being refined and popularized; and a "requiem for democracy" has already been released. The personally benign Professor Skinner has already been attacked as a would-be dictator, an enemy of the people, and as a denigrator at the very least of freedom and dignity, if not of the pursuit of happiness. But despite such criticism, or possibly because of it, Skinner's influence has never been stronger than at present. His presuppositions, methodology, and goals are being rigorously examined, and his hope of seeing his approach more widely used and validated has never seemed more likely to be fulfilled. Some of the moral implications of Skinner's ideas on utopian planning are examined in this volume by Melvin Schuster.

Another sign of the resurgence of utopianism is the commune movement. Since 1960 there have been more utopian intentional communities founded in this country than at any other time since the nineteenth century, when utopian communes sprang up from Massachusetts to California. A recent estimate puts the number at about 2,000, each of which has its own unique problems, goals, and ideational commitments ranging from Cyrenaic hedonism to Christian asceticism. Disenchanted with the established American way of life, impatient with traditional modes of change, critical of materialism and affluence, countless Americans are returning to the land in search of alternative life styles, many of which reflect a desire for a renewed sense of community. War, pollution, crime, inequality and sexual repression are inevitable effects, many of these people believe, of a society that has relied too long on science and technology to solve all its problems, and has failed to put into effect the radical social measures that would make possible the emergence of a new consciousness and with it a new social order. Perhaps pilot utopian experiments can develop solutions to human problems on a smaller scale, and point the way for the larger society to follow. But in order to do this, as Joseph Wellbank points out in this volume, they must themselves show greater awareness of "the constraints of justice."

This utopian hope is nothing new. It was also characteristic of many of the nineteenth century communal experiments, such as the Shakers and Robert Owen's New Harmony, and of the transcendentalist communes, Fruitlands and Brook Farm. What is new is the context within which the current communal movement is taking place. The "global village" made possible for the first time by the mass media, the new scientific techniques which are making many of the pipe-dreams of previous utopian planners (e.g. eugenics programs, behavioral engineering) seem quite feasible in the near future, the scientific study of what has and has not worked in previous utopian experiments, the wider recognition of the ecological crisis, the possibility of an atomic war that may put an end to civilization—these are some of the factors which have made more people take seriously the efforts of the "new utopians."

Another sign of utopian mentality, the experimental attitude toward morality which philosophers such as John Dewey and Bertrand Russell advocated long ago, has also become quite common among today's communitarians. Experiments in free love and group marriage have been tried in attempting to find alternatives to the nuclear family. By no means all communitarians agree on the value of such experimentation. "Jesus people" communes, for example, have usually followed earlier monastic and ascetic traditions of utopian living, condemning promiscuity, supporting the nuclear family, forbidding the use of drugs, and stressing the importance of hard work and postponement of gratification in directing energies toward spiritual perfection and ultimate salvation. Many other communards, however, have discarded the work ethic and sexual repression along with the Protestant ethic with which these have long been associated, and in their place have put the values of immediate gratification and communal sharing. Drug taking has also become widespread in many communes, sometimes just for pleasure but also as a means of altering consciousness and expanding awareness to reveal new ways of growth. In this volume Walter Clark explores the relationship between drug taking and utopianism.

In the current stage of development of our post-industrial society, more attention can be paid not only to the community of interests but to their diversity. As Alvin Toffler points out in *Future Shock* (1970), we have reached a point economically and socially where uniqueness and diversity are more valued than standardization and conformity. This too is in harmony with the spirit of utopianism. Minority groups are more outspoken in their demands and are getting a wider and often more sympathetic hearing. Blacks demanding a larger share in the national prosperity, women raging at being exploited, Indians claiming their rights as original Americans, Chicanos clamoring for freedom to work unhampered, homosexuals protesting against discrimination—these and other previously silent or silenced groups are now eagerly giving vent to their frustrations and airing their complaints, which are often adjoined with utopian proposals. In this volume Preston Williams sets forth a Black perspective on utopianism.

These, then, are some of the signs of our times which suggest a resurgence of utopianism despite the pessimism of dystopians. New images of man, such as those discussed in this volume by Doris and Howard Hunter, are emerging in literature and cinema. The polarity which the Hunters analyze and discuss in "*Siddhartha* and *A Clockwork Orange*," that of immediate enlightenment versus "ultraviolence," continues to draw contemporary youth in two different directions. At one moment their hopes for utopian fulfillment and complete awareness are aroused and at the next moment they are crushed, making violence—creation through destruction—more attractive and, to some, justifiable.

The utopian "new man" has not yet emerged in America, although Charles Reich in *The Greening of America* (1970) has adumbrated his image: a person capable of sensitivity and compassion without fear of being called effeminate, willing to work heroically when he thinks it worthwhile and to loaf sublimely without guilt when he wishes, master rather than slave of machines, ecstatic over sunflowers as well as sex, at peace with his fellow man, filled with a sense of organic social solidarity and, most important, creative, happy, free. This utopian image of man, and Reich's argument that the new generation reflects it, has aroused considerable controversy. The validity of the author's logic, his interpretation of American social history, the feasibility of a non-violent revolution, the meaning and value of the counterculture, and the intentions and actions of contemporary youth have been subjects for fruitful but inconclusive debate. Is the paradigm of American youth to be a "tuned-in" Siddhartha, a Consciousness III Sir Galahad, or— among numerous other possibilities—a "turned off" but ultra- violent Alex, hero of *A Clockwork Orange*? Utopian and dystopian literature may help us to answer this question, or at least help us avoid future shock. "Utopia," wrote Victor Hugo, "is the truth of tomorrow."

Ethics, Utopia And Dystopia

A wide range of interrelated ethical concerns are discussed in the various essays in this volume. Although the examples used are often topical, the basic issues are perennial moral preoccupations.

The Nature of Justice and Human Rights

The definition of justice and the discussion of its social and moral implications have been major concerns of moral philosophers from Plato to John Rawls. Using the United Nations' Bill of Rights as a touchstone for his discussion, J. H. Wellbank shows why an adequate conception of social justice is of crucial importance to utopian speculation and planning. He also shows how, when utopians fail to take into account the specific demands or constraints of social justice in their design and implementation of a culture or an intentional community, they run into serious moral inconsistencies which their enemies, including dystopians, can justly criticize and satirize. Wellbank's article can help us to judge more clearly and critically current utopian experiments and proposals insofar as they promise the best kind of community; all too often they promise happiness without paying sufficient attention to the rights of all their members, especially children.

In "Black Perspectives on Utopia," Preston Williams also focuses on justice and the rights of "life, liberty and the pursuit of happiness" in discussing the Black quest for an improved and more truly democratic society. After tracing the Black Americans' utopian dreams back to their first authentic manifestations in Negro spirituals, Williams looks briefly at Black communal experiments of the post Civil War period, which aimed at educating ex-slaves for freedom, and at four of the Black utopian visions of the twentieth century: those of Marcus Garvey, Father Divine, the Black Panthers, and the Black Muslims. But these utopian visions, Williams points out, have not succeeded in capturing the imagination or expressing the spiritual aspirations of the whole Black Community as fully and dynamically as the utopian dreams and efforts of Martin Luther King, Jr. Freedom, dignity, the extension of democratic government and economic opportunity, and a stress on universal brotherhood and peace were central themes in King's ideal society and remain important ingredients in the Black vision of utopia as Williams interprets it.

Moral Ends and Technical Means

The impact of scientific and technological progress upon the definition of the good life and the quest for utopia, a topic of great interest to contemporary philosophers, is discussed by Walter Fogg in "Technology and Dystopia." Fogg first re-counts the development of utopian hopes for a perfect techno-logically-based society from Francis Bacon's *New Atlantis* (1627) through the Industrial Revolution, then traces their decline as dissatisfaction with industrial society grew and at-tacks upon it mounted. The dystopias of the twentieth century, Fogg goes on to show, reflect increasing disenchantment with a life governed by mechanization and regimentation as well as a disturbing awareness that the human price to be paid for utopia might be far too great. If nature must be ruthlessly mutilated and man and society completely manipulated in order to reach uto-pia, is it really worth attaining? Technological visions of the future are by no means lacking today, Fogg realizes, but in his opinion "traditional utopian literature seems curiously irrele-vant to our times." The important normative questions have been raised by utopians and dystopians, but "future shock" pre-vents us from discovering relevant answers.

Moral and Political Commitment and Action

Assuming that one has determined the ends of the good life, how are they to be achieved? In "Skinner and the Morality of Melioration" Melvin Schuster places B. F. Skinner's approach to utopian planning in the context of a tradition in moral philoso-phy which goes back to Plato and Aristotle; a tradition of meliora-tion, which sets as the prime end of political action human perfectibility, "the improvement of man and the creation of the good life." Schuster carefully sets forth the Skinnerian utopian *Weltanschauung*—its central values, its faith in operant condition-ing, its acceptance of determinism, and its reliance upon the principle of expert authority for leadership and control, i.e. its elitism. Schuster directs his (and our) attention away from the current preoccupation with Skinner's goals and his rejection of freedom and dignity. He urges that we instead examine carefully Skinner's "Meliorative hypothesis" upon which his whole approach stands or fails. This Schuster finds reason to reject. Whether or not one agrees with his position, Schuster's analysis should help one to understand better and to view more critically Skinner's proposed behavioral engineering as a road to utopia.

Alienation and De-alienation

In setting forth and criticizing Marxist utopian views, Pavel Kovaly focuses on a problem which not only Marx and Engels but also other moral philosophers quite different from them—Plato, Hegel, Fromm, and Dewey—have analyzed and attempted to solve, the problem of alienation. As Kovaly points out, Marx and Engels believed that the alienation of the worker from the products of his labor, from his fellow man, and from himself would end only with the abolition of private property and the triumph of the communist revolution. A new completely de-alienated man, the product of a classless society, would eventually emerge. But, as Kovaly goes on to argue, the abolition of private property and the dictatorship of the communist party, with its subsequent concentration of enormous power, has not led to de-alienation of the workers but has preserved and in some ways increased their alienation. Also, contrary to the utopian vision of Marx and Engels, the state, far from showing signs of withering away, remains a source of repression and absolute control. For these and other reasons—for example, the communist use of immoral means to achieve moral ends—Kovaly finally takes a distinctly dystopian view of the communist utopia. Kovaly shows that he is vitally concerned, like Wellbank, with the moral judgment of utopian plans and with viewing utopias in light of "the constraints of justice."

Ideals of Human Nature

Attempts to define and understand human nature, to judge human conduct according to moral norms, and to conceive of

an ideally perfected humanity have long occupied moral
philosophers, especially utopians. Man's quest for psychic
wholeness is the central theme of Doris and Howard Hunter's
essay "*Siddhartha* and *A Clockwork Orange.*" Searching for
unity of selfhood, individuals confront polarities, not only
good and evil, hope and despair, pleasure and pain, but also
harmony with an externally defined social order as opposed to
identity with an inwardly defined ideal of self, which often
demands external non-conformity and sometimes rebellion. It
is this latter polarity, the Hunters believe, which accounts for
two quite different kinds of utopia, outward and inward
directed. They proceed to discuss the heroes of *Siddhartha*, the
novel by Hermann Hesse, and *A Clockwork Orange*, the novel
by Anthony Burgess and the film by Stanley Kubrick, as motivated by the search for authenticity while disturbed by inner
conflicts. But whereas Siddhartha wins his way through to
human wholeness through identifying with an inwardly defined
heaven on earth, Alex in *A Clockwork Orange* rebels against
the demands of an outwardly directed social order, which Burgess depicts as dystopian, finds outlet for his creative spirit
by vicious destructiveness, is temporarily reconditioned to conform to society, and finally reverts to impotent rage. The Hunters' subtle analysis of these two important images of man can
profitably be related to other topics discussed in other essays in
this book, especially Schuster's discussion of Skinner's melioristic ethic, Wellbank's discussion of justice, and Kovaly's discussion of alienation.

Moral Awareness and Relationship

Awareness of oneself as a moral agent with extensive moral
relationships and responsibilities has long been a topic for critical
reflection in ethics. The moral implications of taking psychedelic drugs, chemical agents which can heighten awareness by
altering consciousness, and which can, in Walter Clark's view,
release religious experience, have recently been widely discussed. As an experienced and sympathetic observer of the
psychedelic and utopian scene and as a moral philosopher,
Clark traces the current interest in drugs to their alleged ability
to increase and intensify love, the appreciation of nature, and

metaphysical and religious interests. While Clark does not overlook the sometimes dystopian aspects of psychedelic communes—bad drugs and bad drug experiences, for example—he feels that often these problems are aggravated by a lack of understanding and sympathy on the part of outsiders and by the threat of punitive measures by hostile external authorities. Even those readers who may find much to disagree with in Clark's views on the value of psychedelic agents will probably agree with his view that they have released new influences in our society which deserve serious attention. Moral philosophers will not want to leave psychedelics only to chemists, psychologists, policemen and politicians to appraise, when their use affects moral conduct and leads to consequences which may be judged to be either good or bad.

From the above discussion one can gather that the issues centering around the topic "Utopia/Dystopia?" are manifold and complex, as our authors will show in their various articles. To the student of ethical problems the study of utopias and dystopias offers fascinating material for reflection and analysis. Every utopia and dystopia offers a vision of the good life, a conception of ideal human conduct and of the norms by which it can be achieved and regulated, and often explicit or implicit solutions to moral problems including general problems such as freedom and evil as well as more specific problems such as euthanasia and abortion. In the case of dystopia the vision is often presented in distorted or indirect manner, but the vision of the good life is there, just as happiness missed is always present, as Arthur Miller points out, in the background of every tragedy. Every author of a dystopia, like every author of a utopia, pronounces a moral judgment upon the society in which he lives. We may not agree with his judgment or understand its rationale at first, but we can profit a great deal if, like the earth child hero of Robert Heinlein's *Stranger in a Strange Land*, we "grok" it.

Utopia and Dystopia:
A Look Backward
GLENN NEGLEY

THE LIMITATIONS and the repetitive impact of ordinary language tend to create the illusion that in the coinage and propagation of a new linguistic expression we have discovered or created a new factual configuration. So it would seem to be with our current expression "the Establishment"; the sharpest divisions of contemporary opinion are apparently derived from support of or opposition to this often ill-defined Establishment.

Utopian and dystopian reaction to the Establishment is nowhere better illustrated than in the history of utopian literature. Such writings illustrate vividly that: (1) since the earliest social organization, the Establishment has represented the prevailing and restrictive structure of a particular society; (2) the Establishment represents a monopoly of power entrenched in the *institutions* of that society; (3) political, economic, religious, and cultural controversy has generally been within the framework of utopian-dystopian attitudes toward the dominant Establishment.

Glenn Negley is Professor of Philosophy at Duke University and co-editor of *The Quest for Utopia*.

Wherever one may concede that utopian speculation began, Plato is a convenient and proper reference to origins. If ever there was an Establishment man, it was Plato; to be sure, it was *his* Establishment he wanted, and in all of political literature there is hardly a more carefully and precisely devised plan of a state Establishment than is to be found in the *Laws*. A much more important work than the more popular *Republic*, it has yet to be properly appreciated for Plato's prescience in regard to the dominance of administration, i.e. bureaucracy, in any state Establishment[1]. Almost immediately, Plato's utopian ideas were satirized in dystopian reaction, especially by Aristophanes in *The Ecclesiazusae*, establishing a pattern that was to be rather common in subsequent literature, *e.g.*, the numerous satires of Bellamy's utopian vision.[2] Thus we may remark the rather odd circumstance that the utopian's reaction to the Establishment is often the subject of someone else's dystopian reaction to his own proposed utopian Establishment.

The Establishment can therefore be used almost as a definitive term in historical retrospect and appraisal of utopian thought. The long centuries of relatively quiescent acceptance of the Establishment marked also an almost complete absence of utopian works in Western literature. The revival of antagonism to the Establishment in the 17th century immediately produced one of the most intriguing, influential, and diverse centuries of utopian writing. During this period of extensive and profound literary activity, the various reactions to the old Establishment and to proposals for a new Establishment present a pattern for the history of utopian speculation. *Utopia* was of course a precedent; Thomas More was dystopian toward the Establishment against which he inveighed, but he *apparently* proposed an Establishment of his own making which was indeed very rigid and inflexible by any standards.[3] The "return to nature" theme of *Utopia* was prophetic; how influential it was in the rising tide of thought in the 18th century is debatable (see discussion below). At any rate, the utopians of the 17th century, perhaps the most important century in utopian thought, were on the whole Establishment men. They were interested, as was Plato, in putting forward their own structure of the Establishment—but it *was* an Establishment. In short, their utopian perspective was focused on the improvement, not the destruction, of institutions, the ideal of an Establishment which would provide man the opportunity to achieve and maintain the potentialities of wisdom, fraternity, and freedom of which he was capable—given an appropriate social structure and organization.

The proposals of these 17th century utopians for an Establishment that would satisfy the demands of humanity were fundamentally as far-reaching, varied, and controversial as those which have been explored in the subsequent three hundred years. Tommaso Campanella, in his *City of the Sun*,[4] described an Establishment that could serve as a model of totalitarian society if any dictator were sufficiently subtle and cunning to achieve Campanella's insidious institutional organization. The tortuous agony of individuals in Orwell's *1984* is less horrible to contemplate than the institutional, hierarchical system of "confessionals," in which Campanella utilized the awesome power of religion to achieve an absolute consolidation of power in a dictator "priest" of tyrannical authority, assisted by a self-perpetuating politburo of three "high priests." Translated in these terms, Campanella may not have meant quite this extreme of hierarchical power, but his obsession for the achievement of "law and order," indeed for a Universal Establishment (generated by his reaction to the chaotic and lawless regime of his own Establishment) blinded him to the destruction of the values of individual freedom and expression that were probably his fundamental concern. He was an apostle of the view that the end justifies the means, and he sometimes seems more Machiavellian than the Prince himself. At different times, he was prepared to embrace the Papacy, the Spanish monarchy, and the French nation as the means to his end, the Universal Establishment. However unsatisfactory his speculations were, it is deplorable that they should have cost him terms of imprisonment and considerable torture.

Freedom through dictatorship—maximum freedom in an Establishment of maximum restraints—is an old theme, and an ever-recurring one. Utopian literature abounds with examples of this notion that the final achievement of individual values can be accomplished only by a "temporary" relinquishment of the monopoly of power to a "benevolent" dictator. However, if one considers Campanella's Establishment rigid, censorious, and destructive of individual values, one should at the same time note the reiteration of this dire analysis in utopian writings of the late 19th and early 20th centuries; the dim view of Edward Mandell House (intimate advisor to President Woodrow Wilson) is a particularly interesting example.[5] More nearly parallel to the "utopia" of Campanella is the utilization of the devious devices of contemporary psychology to achieve a kind of final brainwashed degradation in *Walden Two*;[6] Campanella could hardly match the almost hysterical glee of the self-appointed dictator of this community when he acclaims himself a modern-day Jesus Christ. Men will play God—and especially in utopia!

What is perhaps the finest dystopia of the 17th century, *Advices From Parnassus*, was written by a contemporary of Campanella, Traino Boccalini;[7] unhappily this work has suffered almost complete neglect. Boccalini's witty and sophisticated dystopian classic was directed against the influence of the Spanish Establishment in Italy, the Inquisition, and the extension of Papal power. In its day the work was widely known, translated, reprinted, and imitated; numerous references attest the influence of the work on English literature. Witty as it was, however, Boccalini's dystopian invective was ill-received, and it is almost unmistakable that shortly after he moved to Venice he was poisoned by assassins in the hire of the Establishment he criticized; ironically, the constitution and government of Venice were the only Establishment for which he had any admiration.

The Establishment of Venice was also the model for the most influential utopia of this utopia-oriented 17th century: *Oceana*, by James Harrington.[8] Again, it is somewhat incredible that this man and his utopian projections should have been so neglected in subsequent historical evaluation, for it is unquestionable that the Establishment pictured by Harrington in *Oceana* and *The Rota* was the single most influential source in the establishment of the Constitution of the United States. Only in historical retrospect can we appreciate how revolutionary and "utopian" in the 17th century were some of the principles of Harrington's Establishment. The ballot as statutory method of election to the governing body (not to come in England for almost two hundred years); an elective senate and a popular assembly; an agrarian law abolishing primogeniture; limitation of the amount of property to be owned by an individual—these were still radical ideas when they were being considered by our "founding fathers" over a hundred years later. Harrington's prescience is attested by the fundamental principle of his political philosophy, that the economic Establishment is the controlling factor in any social structure and that therefore the economic Establishment must be regulated by the political Establishment. This very modern view is also reflected in the brief and somewhat whimsical utopian excursion of Robert Burton, "An Utopia of Mine Own."[9]

The technological utopia also had its 17th century spokesman—Bacon, of course, in his *New Atlantis*.[10] The potentialities of scientific research and application are presented as restructuring an Establishment based on superstitution, ignorance, and the obscurantism of theology. His projections, from the rather meager data of his day, were unusually astute, although commonplace today, including his anticipation of the laser beam. Widespread scepticism about the promise of an acceptable technological Establishment is unquestionably one of the main sources of our contemporary social malaise, but Bacon's utopia was only the first in a long line of projected Establishments which sought the ideal in a scientific, technological, computerized future.[11]

Finally, the relation of the sexes—a major problem for most utopians, past and present—was resolved in this fertile 17th century by, of all persons, a monk, Gabriel de Foigny.[12] *Terra Australis Incognita* is a country of hermaphrodite nudists living in a state of natural simplicity and innocence. If by chance a child of only one sex was produced, it was immediately strangled as a monster. This dystopian fantasy has been interpreted in several ways: as the work of a debased rascal, a forefunner of the "return to nature" philosophy, and as a satire on the Establishment of 17th century France.

Whatever may have been Foigny's intent and influence, it is certainly historical fact that the acceptance of *some* Establishment which characterized almost all utopian writing of the 17th century was to suffer an abrupt and startling rejection for approximately the next one hundred and fifty years. It is appropriate that this change of pace should have been heralded by a utopia published at the end of the century in 1699, *The*

Adventures of Telemachus, by Francois Fenelon.[13] The work
is a very confused jumble of ideas, as confused as some contemporary social speculation, and for the same reason. Fenelon
describes two societies, one a natural, simple, and uninstitu-
tionalized arcadia, the other a highly institutionalized Establishment of trade and commerce. The best that can be said of
Fenelon is that he well marks the transition from pro-Establish-
ment to anti-Establishment, for he wants the best of both worlds.

Thus the long anti-Establishment era of the "commune" was
ushered into the utopian drama. This development portrays
both the utopian and the dystopian: dystopian in its general
and often bitter rejection of the contemporary Establishment,
or indeed of any Establishment at all; utopian in that it idealized
the natural rationality and beneficence of man uncorrupted by
a corrupt Establishment. This stage of literary effulgence exploited the virtues of the "natural" as compared to the iniquities
of the institutional. Too, the historical time was ripe for a real
exploration of the practical possibilities of realizing utopia;
more than one hundred and fifty such communitarian ventures
are recorded during the 18th and early 19th centuries in North
America.[14]

The ideal of the anti-Establishment persists in our speculation and practice; but so does the ideal of an Establishment
which will confer the "blessings" of technology or law and
order or political stability or digital computerized nonentity.

NOTES

1. See Glenn R. Morrow, *Plato's Cretan City* (1960). Nobody should venture
statements about Plato's political philosophy without acquaintance with Morrow's scholarly appraisal.

2. *E. g.*: Richard C. Michaelis, *Ein Blick in die Zukunft* (1890); William Mor-
ris, *News from Nowhere* (1890); J. W. Roberts, *Looking Within* (1893); Arthur D.
Vinton, *Looking Further Backward* (1890); Conrad Wilbrandt, *Des Herrn
Friedrich Ost Erlebnisse in der Welt Bellamy's* (1891).

3. What Sir/St. Thomas really meant remains a matter of controversy. Russell
Ames summarizes fourteen of the more common interpretations of *Utopia* in
Citizen Thomas More and his Utopia (1949).

4. *Civitas Solis* in *Realis Philosophiae Epilogisticae* (1623). Until recently,
The City of the Sun was available only in the poor and badly abridged translation of Thomas W. Halliday; a much more accurate and meaningful translation
is that of William J. Gilstrap in *The Quest for Utopia*, by Glenn Negley and
J. Max Patrick (1952, 1962, 1971). The most exhaustive work in English on

Campanella, with an excellent bibliography, is *Tommaso Campanella: Renaissance Pioneer of Modern Thought*, by Bernardino M. Bonansea (1969).

5. *Phillip Dru: Administrator* (1912). See also *e. g.*: George G. Hastings, *The First American King* (1904); William Salisbury, *The American Emperor* (1913); Louis Tracy, *An American Emperor* (1897); Newman Watts, *The Man Who Could Not Sin* (1938).

6. By B. F. Skinner (1948).

7. *De' Raguaggli di Parnaso* (1612, 1613); *Advices from Parnassus . . . Revis'd and Corrected by Mr. Hughes* (1706). The best study of the work in English is that of Richard Thomas, "Trajano Boccalini's 'Raguaggli di Parnaso' and its influence upon English literature," in *Aberystwyth Studies*, vol. III, 1922. Another amusing dystopia of the period, though not as pointed as Boccalini's, is *Mundus Alter et Idem*, by Joseph Hall (1605); *The Discovery of a New World*. Ed. Huntington Brown (1937).

8. *The Common-Wealth of Oceania* (1656); *The Rota* (1660). See Charles Blitzer, *An Immortal Commonwealth* (1960); Zera Fink, *The Classical Republicans (1945); H. F. Russell-Smith, Harrington and his Oceana* (1914).

9. The Preface to *The Anatomy of Melancholy* (1621); expanded in later editions.

10. *New Atlantis. A Worke Unfinished* (1626; probably written 1612-13).

11. See especially the numerous utopian works of H. G. Wells.

12. *La Terre Australe Connue* (1676).

13. *Suite du Quatrieme Livre de l'Odysee d'Homere, ou les Aventures de Telemaque, Fils d'Ulysse* (1699). The popularity of this work is inexplicable; the Catalogue Generale of the Bibliotheque Nationale (1929) lists over 700 entries in 14 languages.

14. See Arthur E. Bestor, *Backwoods Utopias* (1950); Mark Holloway, *Heavens on Earth* (1951); Charles Nordhoff, *The Communistic Societies in The United States* (1875).

Utopia and the Constraints of Justice

JOSEPH H. WELLBANK

"Justice . . . that cautious, jealous virtue."

David Hume

"Justice is the first virtue of social institutions, as truth is of systems of thought."

John Rawls

"You have only to be sufficiently determined to realize heaven on earth to be sure of raising hell."

H. D. P. Lee

IF TRAGEDY IS THE CONFLICT between good and good, rather than simply between good and evil, as Hegel somewhere suggests, then the tragedy in many a utopian vision is the implicit moral conflict between the proposed ideals for the good life and the jealous demands of justice. A failure to meet these demands in a society patterned after, say, Bellamy's *Looking Backward*, can give rise to the repressive hedonism of Huxley's *Brave New World*, or it can turn Skinner's *Walden Two* into a Zamiatin *We*. More precisely, if the demands of justice are ignored, the "good place" (EUTOPIA) portrayed in a constructive utopia can turn into the "no place" (UTOPIA) of a satire, or worse, it can degenerate into the "bad place" (DYSTOPIA) of the anti-utopia or dystopia.

What, then, are the demands of social justice, that is, the rights and duties we have as social beings, that provide the moral parameters for constructive utopian thought and action, or, failing to achieve that, which give moral bite to the utopian

Joseph H. Wellbank is Associate Professor of Philosophy at Northeastern University.

satirist or lead to the social pessimism of the dystopian? The
aim in this chapter is to make some remarks towards answering
that question and, accordingly, we shall discuss two topics
related to the theme of justice and utopia: (1) the value of an
adequate conception of justice to utopian thinkers and doers,
and (2) a consideration of some specific demands of justice that
seem to run counter to some current utopian trends.

Toward A Conception Of Social Justice

The virtue of justice should not be predicated of a society
simpliciter, since some of its institutions and practices can be
unjust while others are just, or they can be just (or unjust) at
different times, or they might even satisfy the demands of justice
to a reasonable degree. Thus, at the outset we might suspect that
no society in fact or fiction has ever been wholly just nor completely unjust, although some have no doubt come close to either
limit. Whether this observation also applies to the Western
religious conception of Heaven (as the perfectly just place) and
Hell (as a fit or just place for unrepentant sinners) we must leave
for theologians to discuss. In any case, the question of the justice of any real or imaginary society can always be raised, and
that will invariably entail the issue of whether or not its institutions and practices satisfy the demands of justice to some
reasonable degree.

Implicit in the discussion of the justice of this or that institution or practice of a society lies a standard or conception of justice without which no coherent assessment whatever could be
made. A reading of utopias from Plato to the present will show
that some conception of justice is inherent in any criticism of
existing ways of doing things or in proposed changes for social
betterment. Moreover, without a conception of justice to guide
social thought and action, utopian proposals can unwittingly
lead to social injustice if implemented, or can be exploited by
those who would employ the rhetoric of justice in order to gain
and keep power and privilege.

A conception of social justice is of particular value to utopian
thinkers since, among other uses, one can employ it as Plato
does in Book VIII of *The Republic*, wherein a "pathology of
the State" is constructed in which all types of societies are ranked

according to the degree that they approximate an ideal society. In addition, Plato later in *The Laws* translates his own abstract conception of social justice into the concrete terms of proposed changes in institutions and practices. The value of those post-*Republic* utopian proposals lies not only in seeing where Plato had second thoughts since the halcyon days of *The Republic*, but, more importantly, in learning how to apply a conception of social justice to the basic structure of a given society.

Having an adequate conception of social justice should be of the first importance to every serious utopian thinker and practitioner, since it defines what Professor John Rawls calls the basic structure of society, that is, "the way in which the major social institutions distribute fundamental rights and duties and determine the division of advantages from social cooperation."[1] Hence, whatever utopian proposals are made, and regardless of the motives of the utopians or the attractiveness of their ideals, the justice of what they set out to do—in fact or fiction— "depends essentially on how fundamental rights and duties are assigned and on the economic opportunities and social conditions in the various sectors of society."[2]

Granted, then, that any intelligible social criticism and improvement presupposes a conception of justice, *who* is to say what that conception should be? Surprisingly enough, this question is not all that difficult to answer. Rawls has made a convincing case, which we cannot go into here, that all ethical questions are best answered by us to the extent that each of us satisfies the criteria that define competency in moral judges making considered moral judgments.[3] The more difficult question is, *how* can competent moral judges, using their best judgment, arrive at a conception of justice that is not arbitrary in choice, provincial in scope, unduly biased in ideological commitment, or merely serving some vested interests? In other words, the demands of social justice require a conception of justice that is adequate to the human condition wherever and under whatever circumstances human beings find themselves.

Whatever else is expected of a conception of justice, it must at the least: (i) establish the criteria by which genuine demands of justice can be distinguished from specious ones, (ii) provide a theoretical framework in which all genuine demands can be made coherent one with another in the context of the on-going life of a given society, (iii) describe a fair social scheme for the basic structure of a society, and (iv) do all this and more from an impartial standpoint. But how can we hope to reach the impartial standpoint required by the concept of justice, especially if confronted with demands that run counter to deeply felt preferences that are in themselves worthy of achievement? It is so much easier to repudiate or ignore impartiality, accuse everyone of acting on self-interest alone, and then proceed to ignore or redefine the demands of justice to suit our own attitudes and lifestyles. By such means are dystopias and repressive societies born.

Obviously, an adequate theory of justice is not easily constructed and will not be attempted here. In the remainder of this chapter we shall merely consider some of the demands justice can make of utopians.

The Demands Of Justice On A Good Society

"In the name of Justice, we demand . . ." is the formula, and often both the final court of appeal and the prelude to the initiation of force, for changing the *status quo* or for preserving it, for starting revolutions or for stopping them, for writing and building utopias or for ripping them up and tearing them down. The moral force of Justice lies in its dictate: *Pereat mundu, fiat justitia*—"Let Justice reign though the heavens fall," (to which a Talmudic rabbi reputedly offered the rejoinder, "But if the heavens fall, of what use is Justice?").

It is the virtue of justice that makes some demands legitimate and thereby makes resistance to them or subversion of them immoral, even if the result of meeting them should be that some persons lose their possessions, liberties, or even their lives. It seems odd indeed that it could ever be right and just for any human being to lose liberties, possessions, or even life itself, for the sake of others, because such losses are never good in themselves. But Justice is not only jealous of the good achieved by those who do not deserve it, but it will also place severe restrictions upon the pursuit of the good by some if that should lead to an injustice to others. Herein lies the source of the constraints that justice imposes upon all utopian proposals.

The demands of justice are both extensive and detailed, as

even the briefest acquaintance with some of them in such areas as a labor dispute in industry or the civil and criminal proceedings in the Courts will illustrate. Obviously, we cannot consider such details here, but the demands of justice can be seen in a striking way whenever a utopian proposal conflicts with a specific human right. Accordingly, a bill of human rights provides us with a ready-made and manageable list of the kinds of demands justice can make upon the utopian thinker and doer.

The Universal Declaration of Human Rights, promulgated since 1948 by the United Nations and endorsed by each member state, provides as good a list of human rights as one might hope to find.[4] The wording of the U.N. Bill, especially in the Preamble and in Articles 1, 2, and 30, is clearly in terms of the obligatory language of justice. The document should be read in its entirety, but the following excerpts have particular application to utopian proposals, as we shall see later in discussing some specific rights:

> "The General Assembly proclaims this universal declaration of human rights as a common standard of achievement for all peoples and all nations, to the end that every individual and every organ of society, keeping this declaration constantly in mind, shall strive by teaching and education to promote respect for these rights and freedoms and by progressive measures . . . secure their universal and effective recognition and observance, . . .
> "Whereas it is essential . . . that human rights should be protected by the rule of Law, . . .

Articles 1, 2, and 30 set an even more explicit moral context:

> "Article 1. All human beings are born free and equal in dignity and rights. . . .
> "Article 2. Everyone is entitled to all the rights and freedoms set forth in this Declaration, without distinction of any kind, such as . . . political or other opinion, . . . birth or other status . . .
> "Article 30. Nothing in this Declaration may be interpreted as implying for any State, group or person any right to engage in any activity or to perform any act aimed at the destruction of any of the rights and freedoms set forth herein."

The U. N. Bill, then, presents each Right contained therein as a genuine, rather than a specious or even a tentative, demand of justice and as such is binding not only upon all governments and political activists of all ideological stripes, but also upon all utopians whose good intentions and sincerity do not free them from the bonds of Right. Utopians are indeed not immune from committing social injustices, in thought or deed, as we might suspect with Plato's utopian proposal that atheists be put to death, or the decision of many contemporary communards virtually to eliminate privacy, private property, or any feeling and thought that is independent of the group. In fact, utopian proposals should receive a most careful moral examination, since yesterday's utopian proposal can, and in some cases has already, become today's social reality. With these cautions in mind, let us now look at some specific Rights in the U. N. Bill that putatively conflict with some current utopian trends.

"Article 10. Everyone is entitled in full equality to a fair and public hearing by an independent and impartial tribunal, in the determination of his rights and obligations and of any criminal charge against him."

Generally speaking, utopians do not seem to pay much attention to the problem of establishing a fair judicial process in their ideal society, perhaps partly because they expect to use the courts of the "outside" society if the need arises, but more likely because they sanguinely hope that there will be no need for one in the first place. While it is true that some common types of conflicts might well be virtually eliminated in a specific utopia, it by no means follows that all will be, as the following example illustrates.

There is in the State of Virginia a commune patterned after Professor B. F. Skinner's *Walden Two* called *Twin Oaks*.[5] Each member in this commune receives labor credits for work done and every able-bodied person in the community is expected to do his fair share. Apparently, at least two members did not do the work expected of them, and, so far as the facts are clear, the "community" and the "planners" decided that the labor rules had been broken, the accused were brought before them, tried and found guilty, and punished with exile from the commune.

The two defendants in this case might well have some grounds for the charge that their human right to a hearing before an "impartial tribunal" was denied and hence their punishment of exile was arbitrary ("Article 9: No one shall be subjected to arbitrary . . . exile."). It might be said in rebuttal, however, that any institution or group has the right to decide on disciplinary procedures for dealing with recalcitrant members. But that point is true within limits and the U. N. Bill of Rights defines such limits in this case. Moreover, institutions must take care that their procedures do not violate the civil rights of their members. In conclusion, there is a *prima facie* case that *Twin Oaks* falls below the standards of legal justice practiced in contemporary American society and, if that is true, it should take more seriously the right of each of its members to due process.

In debates on matters such as the one raised here it is sometimes argued in rebuttal that society at large too often fails to secure the basic rights of its members, and while that is true, it hardly provides a utopian community the license to ignore civil or criminal rights altogether, or to handle the matter in a slapdash fashion.

If a utopian experiment such as *Twin Oaks* were merely a group of individuals fleeing what they take to be the intolerable living conditions of society at large, it might be thought picayune to take them to task for failing to deal fairly with allegedly recalcitrant members. After all, religious organizations have proceeded in a far more arbitrary manner in handling the same type of problem in many instances. But unlike a religious organization, a genuine utopian experiment presents itself as a paradigm for better social living and so its way of handling problems should be better than, or at least as good as, what is done in the "outside" world. Justice makes stern demands upon those who would carry out their dreams of a better society.

"Article 12: No one shall be subjected to arbitrary interference with his privacy. . . ."

The right to privacy of thought and feeling (and the need for it) seems the most poorly appreciated aspect of human life in many of the communal experiments of the twentieth century. According to Rosabeth Kanter, many nineteenth century utopian communities used all sorts of group techniques to link each person's inner feelings and thoughts to that of the group. Twentieth century communes appear to emphasize this feature even more, through the use of sensitivity training techniques or T-groups and other psychological techniques to ensure conformity with the attitudes and beliefs of the group. The most noticeable exceptions to such practices are found in the anarchistic utopian societies.[9]

The attractiveness of a communal life for some lies in its capacity to bring them happiness and fulfillment in living wholly for a group. By its very nature, privacy and independence in attitude and belief are a threat to a group defining a total way of life for each of its members. In this respect, many twentieth century secular communes differ not at all in form from religious orders (aside, of course, from the celibate tradition of the latter). As such, they infringe on no one's rights, and the dictum, "love it or leave it," aptly applies. But if a commune intends to be utopian, that is, offers itself as a paradigm for society to emulate, then a "love it or leave it" attitude is quite out of place and as morally repugnant as the same attitude found in those who object to any sort of social criticism. A commune that makes every effort within the bounds allowed by the criminal law to control the feelings and beliefs of its members, with the free consent of its members, can be respected (even if not admired) in its life-style. But as a paradigm for a just society, such an ideal is greatly to be feared.

"Article 16:3. The family is the natural and fundamental group unit of society and is entitled to protection by society and the State."

A major characteristic of twentieth century communes is the radical alteration made in family relationships, with the traditional concept of the family replaced by a group of "parents" who usually constitute the entire adult membership of the commune. The patterns of group families vary enormously and for most of them it may be too early to determine whether in fact they will survive, let alone prove psychologically healthy in the long run. On the face of it, a child reared in a commune would seem to have at least as good a chance to emerge as a psychologically healthy adult, as does a child reared in the traditional nuclear family. But psychological questions aside, is there a constraint of justice on familial utopian experiments?

The institution of the family is singled out in the above clause of Article 16 for special protection by society, that is, presumably by public attitudes and opinions, and by the State, that is, presumably by the excercise of the sovereign power of the State. But the Declaration does not specify what definition of the family is intended and the wording of the entire Article is ambiguous (perhaps intentionally so) in that it is applicable equally to group families as well as to the traditional nuclear family. Moreover, no matter how we may privately interpret this right, its final and operative meaning would have to be decided upon by the appropriate governmental body of a people. So far as our own society is concerned, presumably what the law does not forbid is permissible, and hence we can infer that group families are acceptable for those who wish them.

Utopians practicing group family life do seem to run some risk of infringing on the rights of their own children to choose their own pattern of family life upon reaching maturity. It is only natural that a group family would want to see their version of the institution of the family perpetuated in their children. Hence it is to be expected that a child reared in a group family would more than likely have a poor or distorted understanding of traditional family life, with the stresses and strains of the traditional family compared invidiously with those found in the group family. But group families can in their own way be just as repressive of human growth as can the traditional family. The practice of the nineteenth century Oneida commune in preventing people from becoming too fond of each other by allowing each member to have sexual relationships with more than one partner is but one case in point.[7]

If a variety of familial patterns fall within the scope of the human right to found a family, then not only the traditional or nuclear family but the group or communal family as well has an obligation to educate their children in the variety of familial life-styles available in a free society.

"Article 17:1. Everyone has the right to own property alone as well as in association with others."

By their very nature, communes find few if any virtues in private property (as distinct from such personal property as a toothbrush, etc.) and a great many real or imagined evils. We

should bear in mind that no one commits an injustice in waiving
a right to private property, so long as it is done freely and with
full knowledge. However, a commune developing a specific
life-style expressing merely the freely-arrived-at preferences of
its members is one thing, and an utopian experiment is quite
another. It is hardly ideal in a free society for individuals to be
denied the opportunity, and hence the right, to own property
alone if they themselves do not wish to live under communal
conditions. In this respect, a commune that abolishes the right
to own property alone, while within its right to do so, is dystopian rather than utopian if its practice is presented as an ideal
for society at large.

Conclusions

The following conclusions are drawn from the brief consideration given above to the demands that justice makes upon
utopias.

1. A conception of justice, that is, a justifiable account of our
rights and duties as social beings, is a prerequisite for any
utopian thought and action worthy of our attention.

2. Constructive utopias and utopian experiments need to be
more sensitive to the demands of justice, and in particular to
human rights, if they hope to create social ideals suitable for a
free and just society. A failure to take seriously the demands of
justice not only invites the high risk of creating an unjust
society, but, so far as utopian literature is concerned, invites
the ridicule of the satirist and the censure of the dystopian.

3. Many contemporary communal experiments might be better
conceived of as clubs or "monastic" communities rather than as
utopias. So conceived, justice might make little or no demands
upon them. But if such experiments are meant to be utopian,
that is, to create paradigms for "outside" society to emulate,
then they may well be exercises in creating institutions and
practices that deny the fundamental rights and freedoms of
human beings.

4. Finally, and perhaps most importantly, very little attention
seems to have been given to the rights of children in contemporary communal experiments. It would be a violation of Article
30 of the U. N. Bill if any group, utopian or otherwise, so reared

children that they grew up ignorant of or were led to despise specific human rights. Yet many contemporary communal experiments appear to be moving precisely in this direction, especially in connection with the rights discussed in this chapter. The life of a child should include more than love and happiness. No doubt some Hitler Youth or the children of black slaves on some Southern plantations had at least that much. The life of a child should include an opportunity to grow into the full enjoyment of the rights and freedoms to which a human being is entitled. And that, at the least, is what utopia is all about.

NOTES

1. John Rawls. *A Theory of Justice*, Cambridge, Mass: Harvard University Press, 1971, p. 7.

2. *Ibid.*

3. For a detailed discussion of these criteria, see John Rawls, "Outline of a Decision Procedure for Ethics," *Philosophical Review*, LX (1951), 177-97.

4. A copy of the U. N. Bill of Rights can be found in any public library. It should also be mentioned that each member State has signed the Declaration but none has signed the Covenant of Human Rights. The latter would make each Right listed in the U. N. Bill the positive law of each signatory State. Communal experimenters might have cause to worry if this Bill of Rights ever became the law of the land.

5. See Kathleen Kinkade, *A Walden Two Experiment: The First Five Years of Twin Oaks Community*. New York: William Morrow, 1973.

6. Rosabeth Kanter. "Communes." *Psychology Today*. July, 1970, p. 55.

7. *Ibid.*

Black Perspectives on Utopia
PRESTON N. WILLIAMS

ANY REFLECTION UPON THE LIFE of blacks in America leads one to conclude that their experience would naturally have prompted the development of both utopian and dystopian reflection. Utopian vision arose from the wretched condition of the black person in America. Deprived of life, liberty, and the pursuit of happiness by the founding fathers, his daily existence was a contradiction of all white America had to say about the value and worth of persons. Yet while whites denied his personhood and made him, according to law, custom, and usage, property, the black American experienced in his own flesh and soul the full humanity of every human being. Blacks certainly then envisioned a better future for themselves and America. They dreamt of a changed disposition on the part of white persons, an overcoming of slavery and racial prejudice and discrimination, and the creation of more perfect communities. Utopian visions must have entered their thought, buoyed up their hopes, and nourished their efforts at social change. Similarly the

Preston N. Williams is Houghton Professor of Theology and Contemporary Change at the Harvard Divinity School.

realities or rumors about slave life in the Deep South, the harsh-
ness of the Black Codes and Fugitive Slave laws, must have
brought forth notions of dystopia. Whites, when they used their
imaginations to speculate about the perfect society, quite frequently saw the new order as a more adequate suppression of
the Negro or a removal of him to another continent. For many
a black person this mode of thinking led to the embracing of
dystopian feelings. The white American's utopia was opposed by
blacks, not because the latter did not want change but because
they could not secure the type of change they sought in America.
Ideal life for whites meant complete dehumanization of blacks,
and blacks thus came to desire a less perfect white country and
a bit more freedom, if not dignity, for themselves.

Given the oral character of much of black history in America
and the neglect of investigation into black intellectual history,
it is impossible for me to present here a comprehensive statement outlining black perspectives on Utopian and Dystopian
schemes. I will seek rather to suggest what can be learned from
examining one body of materials, the Spirituals, and I shall
compare the findings with some of what we know about black
utopian communities prior to the ending of the Civil War.
Suggestions will then be made about how these visions cor-
respond to and differ from the dream of the Black American
community as expressed by Martin L. King, Jr.

Spirituals and Black Utopianism

I have chosen to examine the Spirituals because I believe
with James Weldon Johnson that the songs are solely the
creation of the American Negro and that preserved in them are
the Negro's native African instinct and talent.[1] While they
reflect the creative powers of unknown single individuals, they
did at the time of origin and still today embody the thought
pattern of the black community.[2] The dominance in the songs
of a Christian symbolism is important because it indicates that
the slaves had become Afro-Americans and participated to a
degree in the European heritage of white America. Although
the slave may then have been illiterate he was conversant enough
with his new culture to understand partially the myths which
explained its past and determined in a measure his future.

Curiously enough, it was in one of the black utopian communities that whites came to be stirred by the power of the Spirituals and began to carry the message of these songs to the world.[3] But even before these songs were carried beyond the slave communities they had become "the Soul of Black Folks," and it is for this reason that my discussion of black perspectives on utopia begins with them.

It should be noted that utopian thought among blacks is not expressed in any treatise outlining the functioning of some distant commonwealth. There is no Plato's *Republic* or St. Thomas More's *Utopia* or Edward Bellamy's *Looking Backward*. Utopian thought was the creation of individuals, but, as with the spirituals, the authors' names were lost and the ideas became a part of the folklore of the people. Failure to research the works of single authors does not mean that none exist, but rather that on this subject the orientation of the black American when he reflects upon utopianism and dystopianism in his community begins with an analysis of his songs, not only spirituals but also jazz, blues and work songs. In them he discovers the vision of the future.

Because the tradition is deposited in song, there is no single interpretation. From the beginning scholars have quarreled over whether the songs referred to this life or the other world, whether they were songs of protest or escape and accommodation. The quarrel still rages, but fortunately we can speak of black perspectives on utopia without settling upon any one interpretation.[4] The elements in the future vision remain the same whether one sees the songs as this—worldly or other—worldly, protest or accommodation.

The ideal state of society will embody freedom for the Negro whether it be in this life or the next. Israel's, Daniel's, Jonah's deliverance foreshadowed the deliverance of the slave. The oppression of the black American was to be ended by the action of God, for "He's Jus' De Same Today," but also by the action of blacks themselves.[5]

> "De want no cowards in our
> ban', —God's gwine-ter build
> up Zion's walls. We call for
> valiant hearted men, God's
> gwine-ter build up Zion's walls."[6]

Freedom, however, was to be joined to justice, as DuBois indicates:

> "Through all the sorrow of the Sorrow Songs there breathes a hope—a faith in the ultimate justice of things. . . . Sometimes it is faith in life, sometimes a faith in death, sometimes assurance of boundless justice in some fair world beyond. But whatever it is, the meaning is always clear: that sometimes, somewhere men will judge men by their souls and not by their skins."[7]

Justice will embrace more, however, than racial justice. The ethic of the Christian faith will be practiced in its purity. Gambling, lying, back-sliding, grumbling will cease.[8] Hypocrisy will be unmasked.[9] Toil will come to an end and loneliness and trouble cease.[10] God will deliver every man and a classless harmony will come into existence.[11] The quest after the Christlike life will be everywhere manifest.[12] Love, humility, and forgiveness will characterize personal relations[13] and joy and celebration will abound.[14] Most surprisingly for a people thought of as being without family, the desire to be reunited with mother, brother, and sister is a constant feature of the new life.[15] The cruelty of slave existence did not quench the natural expressions of personhood.

Visions of Freedom and Black Utopias

When one looks at the several images used in the spirituals to suggest the utopian vision, one sees clearly that what the slaves wanted was a truly Christian and democratic state. Slavery was to be abolished, persons were to love each other and to have fellowship in harmony in spite of race, class, or other differences. All persons were to possess worth and dignity, a sufficiency of worldly goods, ample time for play and celebration, and a sense of at-homeness in nature and society. The vision is basically a religious-ethical one and little attention is paid to the outlining of man's secular functions in business, government, or science. While it is true that this impression flows quite naturally from our sources, the spirituals, it is also supported by the slave's lack of familiarity with these institutions. The slave's position was in house and field, not in business, industry or government, and while some black persons no doubt came to master knowledge about the latter functions of society, they probably were not sufficient in number to alter the content of the community's conception of utopia.

Great weight is lent our conclusion by the research of William H. and Jane H. Pease in their small volume *Black Utopias*. There it is pointed out that Negro communal experiments in America and Canada had as their chief aim the training of the Negro for complete freedom. Black Americans like white Americans saw the necessity of blacks learning how to succeed in a free, competitive, and self-reliant economic society and to prepare for assimilation into the larger society. The black criticism of the social order had to do with its failure to be inclusive of all persons and not the detailed conception of institutional functioning. Theirs was a criticism that struck at the wedding of universalistic thinking to the parochial interest of white groups within America.

Being an "out-class" in the American society, blacks had little experience of the inequities existing in the several institutions of the social order—economic, legal, educational, political. Two consequences followed from this: the black utopia was constructed in a most general fashion and suggested what a transformation of a slave society would mean to oppressed slaves; and the transformed society involved primarily reorientation of values rather than institutional structures. Structural change meant in most instances the opening of the gates to participation by the Negro. The Peases' comparison of white and black utopian communities should not lead one to conclude that blacks sought to maintain the status quo but rather for them the fundamental change had to do not with socialism versus capitalism but slavery versus freedom and black versus white. For the black man utopia in its most profound sense meant freedom, nothing less than free individual choice and decision. There was then a contrast in conception and practice of utopia by blacks and whites, but in both instances the goal was similiar, the greater humanization of mankind.

"The Utopian communities were, by definition, communal in structure and communal in their outlook. They were in the European tradition of socialism and communism. Not so the organized Negro communities. If they partook of any specific social, economic, and political philosophy, it was the philosophy of the

American Middle Class. Far from aiming at a Utopian communal
society, the Negro communities were dedicated to training their
inhabitants in the virtues of self-reliance, individualism, and independence. Economically they operated almost without exception
upon the basis of profit-making capitalism. The Negro communities appeared communal only in the joining of hands in mutual
aid the better to develop the individual; it was not the permanent
fusing of individuals into a truly communal society."[18]

The challenge of the black American's utopia has been lodged
at the roots of America's conception of democracy and religion.
It seeks to create a nation in which all persons could partici-
pate in government, industry and society as free, intelligent
human beings. Racism is to fall before reason and equal opportunity, and the Christian ethic of loving the neighbor as the
self is to prevail. Moreover, the very status of the black man in
America, and the hostility of the white man toward him as
slave or free, means not only loving the neighbor but also
loving the enemy. This concern for radical change led the Negro
to postpone consideration or more detailed questions about the
running of the machinery of government and society.

Black Utopian Movements of the Twentieth Century

To leap from pre-Civil War days to the civil rights era
of the nineteen fifties and sixties is to undertake a broad and
bold jump. This is justified in a discussion of utopian thought
because, of the nine Negro movements and messiahs between
1900-1949, only two, Marcus Garvey and Father Divine, had
real visions of an idyllic new society for blacks.[19] A brief discussion here would render more disservice than service to these
men and their visions. Suffice it to say that Garvey's utopia
would have returned the black Americans to Africa and made
of them a completely African people. While the idea and movement became very popular, it failed completely in its attempt
to persuade black Americans to migrate to Africa or to consider
themselves to be non-Americans. Father Divine's vision was of a
raceless, colorless society which would be universal. In his utopia black would disappear as well as white. While we cannot
discuss it in detail, it should be recognized as an extreme ver-

sion of the classical black perspective on utopia contained in the spirituals. While the Garvey position springs from despair about the future of the Black Americans in America and recommends return to Africa, Father Divine's paradise is built upon a rosy optimism about racial reconciliation in America and elsewhere. In an era of severe economic dislocation he formed new communities of blacks in a group of heavens on earth in several of the larger Americans cities. The communities were to be cooperative; all property and goods were shared; and persons took on a new name to indicate the renewal of themselves. Whites were freely admitted, and following his wife's death Father Divine married a white Canadian. Thus the "kingdom" sought in every way to suggest the new life for blacks and all mankind. Students of utopian thought will want therefore to examine both these movements very closely. They are significant departures from the line of thought we are tracing, but the pattern followed here is the dominant one found among black Americans during the period from the Civil Wat to the present day.

The pre-Civil War period and the period of the fifties and sixties both presaged great changes in race relations resulting from Negro agitation and initiative and cooperation from liberal whites. Moreover, the utopian thought patterns that emerged expressed the majority sentiments of the black American. It is my conviction that black utopian thought is communal even though it may be found in the creation of a single individual or express individualistic elements. The hope is always for an altered status for blacks as a group and not simply as single persons. This community sentiment we see expressed again in song but also in the writings and the leadership of one man, Martin Luther King, Jr.

King's Utopian Dream

The spiritual that best captured revived utopian aspirations and became the anthem of the civil rights revolution was "We Shall Overcome *Someday*." The vision of the new day was vividly pictured in the moving cadence of the "I Have a Dream" speech of Martin King delivered on the steps of the Lincoln Memorial in August of 1963.

"I have a dream that one day on the red hills of Georgia sons of
former slaves and the sons of former slave owners will be able to sit
down together at the table of brotherhood. I have a dream that one
day even the state of Mississippi, a state sweltering with the heat
of injustice, sweltering with the heat of oppression, will be transformed into an oasis of freedom and justice."

"I have a dream that my four little children will one day live in a
nation where they will not be judged by the color of their skin but
by the content of their character."

"When we allow freedom to ring—when we let it ring from every
city and every hamlet, from every state and every city, we will be
able to speed up that day when all of God's children, black men
and white men, Jews and Gentiles, Protestants and Catholics, will
be able to join hands and sing in the words of the old Negro
spiritual 'Free at last, Free at last, Great God a-mighty, We are free
at last.' "[20]

The civil rights conception of utopia remains that of a puri-
fied and Christianized democracy. It is rooted, as King stated, in
the American Dream, but it is not the American Dream.[21] The
American Dream, like the *Republic* of Plato, *Utopia* of More,
and *Equality* of Bellamy,[22] still seems to need a slave class to
shoulder the burden of the new freedom. Blacks are looking for
the fulfillment in a universal republic, of the natural rights of
man as suggested in the phrase of the Declaration of Independence, "life, liberty, and the pursuit of happiness." As W. E. B.
DuBois noted some years ago, their gift is the drive to extend
democracy so that it includes all persons of all colors, creeds, and
conditions of servitude.[23] Now as earlier the vision is rooted in
the concrete experiences of the black American's life. While no
longer considered property, he is not yet fully recognized as
"somebody." Thus the core of the dream remains "freedom
now," but the "now," as the old spiritual suggests, extends
into the distant future—"We Shall Overcome *Someday*." The
relationship between this worldly and other worldly aspirations was manifest even in the most intense direct action cam-
paign of the black American. Martin Luther King frequently
gave voice to this in his references to suffering and death—
themes central to the spirituals—and in his recognition of the
element of code language in the most otherworldly symbols of
the spirituals.[24] The vacillation between this world and the

next, like all else in the vision of utopia, is linked to the concrete experience of blacks in this life. "Freedom Now" gave voice to the impatience blacks experience in the quest for freedom in predominantly white America. "We shall overcome, black and white together. We shall overcome. . . . *someday*" refers to the slow pace of progress blacks feel they have made in the pursuit of human and constitutional rights. Thus the utopian vision builds the hope of the folk upon the possibility of freedom and the reality of freedom delayed. Like the spiritual, the utopian vision urges the people to "Keep a -in-chin along, Keep a -in-chin along, Massa Jesus is coming bye and bye."[25] The substance of the utopian vision is constructed of the best elements of the Christian and democratic promise. Its future would seem to lie in this world, but realism born of experience and the Christian conception of sin lead to the stretching out of the future into the life beyond this life. Thus all blacks, even those who die in hope, may become participants. The formulae "Freedom Now" and "We shall overcome, black and white together . . . *someday*," together with the ambivalent code language of the spirituals, move blacks of every age and condition.

While preserving the main body of traditional thought about utopia, King's vision does add new elements. There is now knowledge about government, business, science, and the internal functioning of society. The new concept of society, while democratic, takes on socialistic ingredients. The black middle class orientation, referred to above, is broken. Blacks go proudly to jail, utilize civil disobedience, employ economic coercion, and talk confidently about a welfare state. Black youth enter the revolution first as allies and then as challengers of their elders. Concern for world peace, the abolition of colonialism, and elimination of poverty at home, is added to the concern for civil and personal rights. All of these were, of course, elements vital to the civil rights revolution. I have placed them in the context of utopian thought because they represent the bold and daring attempt of America's most oppressed minority to save the soul not only of America, but also of much of the world. That the dream was not fully realized in any of its several dimensions does not detract from its audacity. What is central here is that the black extension of democracy in the interpretation of Martin Luther King came to take on more

socialistic and few capitalistic features. This could be attributed
to the Christian doctrine of love of neighbor and not to a commitment to socialism as an economic or political theory. In addition one must note that utopian visions were brought closer
to conceptions of political eschatology. This was due to a systematic strategy devised by King and his followers as well as
to new, courageous and able leaders active in the black community.[26] Despite these changes the main features of utopian
thought among blacks remained unchanged.

Other Black Visions of a New Society

Just as during the period 1900 to 1949, new leaders arose and
sought to change radically the dream of the black community,
so also during the latter days of the civil rights revolution new
messiahs with new visions arose among blacks. The two most
publicized groups of revolutionists were the Black Panthers
and the Black Muslims. The former, despite the implications of
its name, was an integrationist group desirous of reforming
black life as well as American society. Both black and white
worlds were to be remade in the image of Marxism. Although the
group received great attention from white Americans and some
black youth, it did not take root in the black community and
was forced to greatly modify its vision to bring itself into greater
conformity with the classical view.[27]

Unlike the Panthers, the Black Muslim sect did not seek to
replace both the Christian and democratic heritage of blacks.
The group instead emphasized the existing *middle class orientation*, including capitalistic economic views while rejecting the
religious vision of Christianity for that of a distorted Islam. In
addition the group fed upon black frustration and hatred of
whites by describing whites as devils. Unlike Marcus Garvey,
who also preached color caste and sought to establish a black
nation in Africa, the Black Muslims attempted to build a black
nation within the United States of America. While successful
in some of its economic ventures, such as restaurants, super mar-
kets and a newspaper, the Muslim group was unable to win the
hearts of black Americans, and while many blacks were sympathetic toward its economic program and its condemnation of
whites and Christianity, few accepted its vision of the new
society.[28]

Even more significant to the alteration of the black American's perspective on utopia was the decolonization of Africa and Asia following World War II. While this development was in part incorporated into the motivation, strategy, and outcome of the Civil Rights Revolution, its full effect did not come until after the revolution had run its course and its leader Martin King had been martyred. A free Africa seemed to provide blacks with a real option to continued life in America, while at the same time enabling them to recapture their past and become "somebody." Moreoover, the African vision that now filled their dreams had to be recast in the light of the real potentialities of given nations, customs, and people. Fantasy and romanticism could now be restrained or enhanced by actual contact with black Africans. The black man's dream of the future now had to compete with or link itself to the dreams of non-American blacks. In either case a rich new body of resources was put at the disposal of the visionary.

What the new pictures of the future will look like can not be essayed here. The Christian religious base will undoubtedly be expanded to include elements of Islam and African traditional religions. The utopian visions of new governmental, industrial and social institutions will no doubt become more precise and detailed. Most assuredly the main features will continue to be based on a growing appreciation for those black slaves who first sang of freedom and believed in the existence of a power beyond all earthly powers, who fought together with blacks and all others of goodwill for the liberation of all mankind.[29]

NOTES

1. Johnson, James Weldon and Johnson J. Rosamond, *The Books of American Negro Spirituals* (New York City: Viking Compass Edition, 1969), p. 17.

2. *Ibid.*, p. 21.

3. DuBois, W. E. B., *The Souls of Black Folk* (Chicago: A. C. McClurg & Co., 1903), pp. 251-2.

4. For a summary of the various interpretations and a suggestion about the present state of the debate see Cone, James H., *The Spirituals And The Blues* (New York City: The Seabury Press, 1972), pp. 1-34, 108-142.

5. Johnson, J. W. and Johnson, J. R., *Op. Cit.*, Book I, p. 80,60.

6. *Ibid.*, Book II, p. 56.

7. DuBois, W. E. B., *Op. Cit.*, p. 261.

8. Johnson, J. W. and Johnson, J. R., *Op. Cit.*, Book II, pp. 100, 130, 164, 25. Book I, pp. 74, 122.

9. *Ibid.*, Book I, p. 71.

10. *Ibid.*, Book I, pp. 98, 100; Book II, pp. 74, 98, 100, 110, 126, 142, 140, 156.

11. *Ibid.*, Book I, pp. 126, 148.

12. *Ibid.*, Book I, 59; Book II, pp. 133, 160, 166.

13. *Ibid.*, Book I, p. 167; Book II, pp. 72, 74, 86, 183.

14. *Ibid.*, Book I, pp. 71, 162; Book II, pp. 155, 180.

15. *Ibid.*, Book I, pp. 82, 104, 137; Book II, pp. 60, 80.

16. Pease, William H. and Pease, Jane H., *Black Utopias* (Madison: The State Historical Society of Wisconsin, 1963).

17. *Ibid.*, pp. 19-20.

18. *Ibid.*, p. 18.

19. Reid, Ira De A., "Negro Movements and Messiahs 1900-1949," *Phylon*, Volume X, No. 4, Fourth Quarter, 1949, pp. 362-369.

20. Osborne, Charles, *I Have a Dream* (New York: Time—Life Books, 1968), p. 57.

21. *Ibid.*, p. 57.

22. The insistence upon racial prejudice and separation in the ideal state as conceived by Bellamy underscores the radicalness and trans-American nature of the black perspective on utopia. "Even for industrial purposes the new system involved no more commingling of races than the old one had done. It was perfectly consistent with any degree of race separation in industry which the most bigoted local prejudice might demand." Bellamy, Edward, *Equality* (New York: D. Appleton and Company, 1897), p. 365.

23. DuBois, W. E. B., *The Gift of Black Folk*, (New York: Washington Square Press, 1970), pp. 65-67.

24. King, Martin Luther, Jr., *The Trumpet of Conscience* (New York: Harper and Row, 1968), pp. 3-4.

25. Johnson, J. W. and Johnson, J. R., *Op. Cit.*, Book I, p. 134.

26. King was able to enlist a large number of younger and older men to support him in his program. Among these were: Ralph D. Abernathy, Harry Bellafonte, Walter E. Fauntroy, James Lawson, Bayard Ruston, Wyatt T. Walker, and Andrew Young.

27. Forner, Philip S. (ed.) *The Black Panthers Speak* (New York: J. P. Lippincott Co., 1970).

28. Lincoln, C. Eric *The Black Muslims In America* (Boston: Beacon Press, 1961).

29. See Charles H. Long, "Perspectives for a Study of Afro-American Religion in the United States," *History of Religions II* (1971), 54-66.

Technology and Dystopia
WALTER L. FOGG

TECHNOLOGY, broadly defined as skills and practical crafts, goes back as far as the discovery and use of fire, the wheel, the working of metals and the plow. Although the historical origins of *homo faber*, man the toolmaker, are still somewhat murky, man exceeded his natural physical limits by developing his capacity for invention and his techniques for pacifying and exploiting the natural environment. These capacities and techniques also modified his social environment. It was Marx who said that the hand-mill leads to a society of the feudal lord; the steam-mill to a society of the industrial capitalist. But long before Marx gave great impetus to the idea that developing technologies and changing modes of production determine changes in the social order, it was recognized that man's developing skills and inventions had great power to effect social change. In Book II of *The Republic*, Plato saw that specialization of skills and the division of labor were important to the development of society and civilization. Also, in his last work, *The Laws*, Plato, the

Walter L. Fogg is Chairman of the Department of Philosophy and Religion at Northeastern University and co-author, with Peyton E. Richter, of *Philosophy, Looks to the Future*.

social engineer and organizer of Magnesia, a utopian colony in Crete, clearly recognized the socially disruptive effects technology may introduce into his ideal community. Magnesia is to be established nine or ten miles from the sea so that innovations from abroad will not, in a haphazard way, unduly affect the stability and higher moral purpose of the society. The Nocturnal Council, comprised of philosophically minded citizens, is to interpret and review the laws of the society, take charge of the moral education of its citizens, and selectively seek out new knowledge and innovations from other societies. The latter will be introduced into Magnesia in a planned way.

Of course, there are immense differences between Plato's world and ours in almost every respect. The acceleration of technological change has resulted in drastic alterations of our social patterns. We have just begun to understand the complex interface between technology and social change. The problems, at least, are familiar to us: the political issues raised by the threat of nuclear war; the educational issues raised by the use of television and teaching machines; the moral questions generated by developments in biogenetics, organ transplants, and the new drugs; and the ecological and aesthetic questions raised by the unplanned growth of our polluting industries and our agonized cities. But Plato's grasp of the relation between man's developing skills and inventions and their use or abuse in regard to the good of the individual and society seems particularly relevant today. To what extent can societies understand, direct, and control the increasing rate of change being brought about by technology? Can we subordinate technological change to human purposes?

Despite the early optimism about technology and social progress, there is strong opinion in our century, expressed in contemporary dystopias and science fiction, that technology is not only beyond the control of society but that man is still largely unconscious of the profound revolution he is bringing about. In his book, *The Accidental Century*, Michael Harrington states it well:

"The older ideologists and utopians were victimized by their ignorance of the limits of the possible. They sought divine commonwealths and secular salvations which were impossible of achievement. Where these conscious revolutionists of the

past proposed visions which outstripped reality, the unconscious revolutionaries of the present create realities which
outstrip their vision. In the first case, it is history that is sad, in
the second, man."[1]

Technology and Utopia: an Early Optimist

One of the most difficult problems in describing the various
assessments of technology found in utopian and dystopian
literature is the diverse significance "technology" has in these
works. In our day, technology is inseparable from its historical
development, its connection with the industrial revolution and
the economic, social and political history of the West. It is also
inseparable from the development of science since the Renaissance. In the time of Plato, science was mainly a speculative
enterprise which had little connection with the ancient Greek
economy or its practical arts such as medicine or architecture.
The purpose of science for Plato was the contemplation, the
theorectical understanding, of the order of nature. The ancient
Greeks did not recognize an imperative to relate this knowledge
to the harnessing of the powers of nature for the utility of man.
Today science and technology are interdependent. From scientific investigations in such areas as electronics and solid-state
physics, computer technologies have developed. From technological advances such as the development of the electron
microscope and cyclotron have come new discoveries in science.

Given its complex development, there is understandably great
disagreement about the definition of technology. A workable
definition is that technology is an organized and systematic
means of using the materials or forces of nature for the purpose
of producing either useful objects or power to affect man,
society, and nature. The central notions in this definition are
production and utility. Since the rise of modern science in the
Renaissance, the emphasis on the utility of knowledge has been
clearly present. The historical figure who is often cited as being
responsible for the emphasis on the practical and productive
utility of scientific knowledge is Francis Bacon, a seventeenth
century thinker who saw the potentialities of modern science in
its earliest and formative stage. Bacon saw the growth of
scientific knowledge as an historical movement, a collective,

incremental enterprise, a revolution in which man would control nature, reform his fundamental conception of things, and
bring about peace and plenty on earth. Knowledge is power: the
power of invention, discovery, and control.

Bacon was also a utopian writer. He is the prime example
of a utopian who firmly believed that the practical application
of the new science and technology meant the progress of mankind. In his utopia *New Atlantis* (an unfinished work), political
power is in the hands of a group of scientist-engineers (Salomon's
House) who have amassed a considerable number of technological inventions and scientific discoveries. The knowledge gained
through the discovery of the causes and motions of things is to
be used to "enlarge the bounds of the human empire and to effect all things possible." They will have harnessed nature to the
good of the happy island. In Bacon's narrative, one of the members of the House of Salomon enters the town with the solem-
nity of a high priest to tell of wondrous caves he and his co-
workers have established for the purpose of refrigeration and the
conservation of bodies and of the construction of high towers for
the study of the weather. He further extols their capacities to
turn salt water into fresh, their abilities to produce new artificial metals, and their discovery of a Water of Paradise which
is used for health and the prolongation of life. The technological
Establishment has not only sub-divided the scientific labor, they
have separate facilities for experiments in light, sound, smells
and taste. They also have "engine houses" which are used for
the preparation of war, and they have discovered a new mixture
for producing unquenchable wildfires burning in water.

Plato's vision of Magnesia is that of an ideal society whose
main dimensions are ethical and political. He is concerned about
those moral values of the citizens which are formative of stable
personal relations and social structure. Education is central but
it is essentially moral education, education for virtue. Bacon's
New Atlantis, on the other hand, presents us with a society
whose main purpose is discovery and invention. Its orientation
and structure seem more appropriate to a research institute or an
orbiting space lab than to a society in Plato's sense. Its citizens
are aggressively geared to data collecting and attaining power
over the forces of nature. Its appearance is dominated by towers,

machines, experimental apparatus, and statues—not to the gods, but to the major scientist in the society. The underlying purpose of the society is not justice and the Good, but technological productivity.[2]

No other utopian writer matches Bacon's early enthusiasm regarding science and technology. There seems to be no point at which he feels the need to limit its development or its impact on society. But what was "utopian" for Francis Bacon in the seventeenth century was nearly a fact of life by the nineteenth century. Technological change and production had been stimulated by the rise of capitalism. The industrial revolution had begun, and it came to be not only a revolution in the organization of society, but a revolution which profoundly changed the conditions of life for most people. Work and production had moved from the village and the cottage to the large-scale mechanized industry of the big, ugly urban centers. The old crafts were being displaced by the new technical skills essential to inventing and servicing the machine. Technology played a large part in this revolution: the invention of the spinning machine, the development of cast iron, advances in agriculture to meet the new increases in populations, and the tapping of new sources of power such as coal and steam.

Robert Owen's *A New View of Society* reflects these new conditions. Owen, himself a successful factory manager, saw the need to found a new society on sound economic principles, to conbine social reform with economic efficiency. He had first-hand experience of the rampant crime and violence in the urban centers, the use of cruel child labor practices in the factories, and the abject poverty of the worker under a *laissez-faire* capitalism. The new society was to be co-operative and socialistic. The social planner was not to be the philosopher-king of Plato's *Republic* or the scientist-technician of the *New Atlantis*. Rather, the organization of the utopia was to be in the hands of the businessman-technician. Skills necessary to the management of the factory were the skills necessary to run a new society.

Owen came to this country in 1824 to establish a self-sufficient community of 900 people. It was to be a de-centralized, socialistic "community of equality" on 30,000 acres on the banks of the Wabash in Indiana. The Owenites named their first experiment here New Harmony.[3] Although Owen proposed small industrial villages as the ideal social units and placed limits on machine production in each village, he did not directly blame technology and technological change for the failure of his utopia. Many utopian socialists such as Owen pointed to the tragic effects of the organization of a society geared to industrial production. They did not tie these effects directly to science or technology. There is nothing wrong with the advance of technology. Society must be reorganized in order to correct its abuses. The Captains of Industry must accept social responsibility and reform society.

Ambivalence Toward Technology and the Machine

In the Greek myth, Prometheus steals fire from the gods to give it to man. By that act, Prometheus is no longer an instrument of the Gods but a challenge; he brings new power and breaks the old limits, the ancient laws. Prometheus is punished for his *hubris*. In Mary Shelley's story, *Frankenstein* (1818), Dr. Frankenstein, an anatomist, is the creator of a powerful monster who, because he lacks the capacity for love and kindness, destroys his creator and his family and, finally, himself. What is new in this case is no stolen element, but a monster created by means of new scientific techniques; the result is not punishment of the transgressor but wholesale destruction. Shelley's story, coming as it did early in the 19th century, symbolizes the fascination and fear with which man responds to the acquisition of new power. Despite the optimism which arose out of the link between the idea of social progress and developing industrialism, technology, and science in this century, there was an undercurrent of ambivalence toward technology and especially its 19th century symbol, the machine. In the literature of this period there is a host of disasters connected with man-machine relationships: the machine goes beyond the intention of those who created it; the machine is impersonal and indifferent to man's values; the machine is destructive of the sense of community and a source of a sense of alienation for man; human beings are made obsolete by machines.

Samuel Butler's satirical utopia *Erewhon* depicts a society which has some of these fears. Early in the social history of Erewhon, there had occurred a civil war between the machinists and the anti-machinists, won by the latter faction. Hundreds of years later, at the time of the narration of the visitor to Erewhon, there remained copies of a treatise, the "Book of Machines," which had helped to foment the war. It reminded the reader that the development of machines had been alarmingly swift in relation to the development of man. Man must rebel against this infant power lest the machines develop a consciousness of their own, learn to tyrannize over man and reduce him to an "affectionate machine-tickling aphid." It warned that machines such as steam boilers are fed by human stokers, that they eat, as it were, by "mannery," and that man is in danger of being reduced to a function of the machine. After the civil war, all inventions had been forbidden in Erewhon and still were forbidden. The inhabitants were suspicious even of their visitor's watch.[4]

We must mention in this connection William Morris' *News From Nowhere* (1890). Written in partial reaction to Edward Bellamy's utopian novel *Looking Backward* (1888), Morris decries the economy-centered socialistic utopia of Bellamy and extols the virtues of the artisan working directly with nature. Man's work in an ideal society should not be motivated by profit. Work should be performed to enhance human life and happiness. The industrial machine means the destruction of the individual's participation in the making of his world. Morris stresses the humane values over automation, the values of spontaneity and a decentralized society dedicated to spiritual rather than material goals. Morris's utopia puts man into a pastoral setting, with simplified wants and a life unencumbered by the growing complexities of modern society.[5] Morris's rationale for rejecting modern industrial society has similarities to that of Thoreau, who looked upon the increasingly complex world of inventions ("improved means to unimproved ends") as unnecessary. Morris and Thoreau are in a sense the spiritual progenitors of many in our contemporary communes who find in the arts and crafts an expression of their preferred life style and their wish to simplify.

The authors I have mentioned are representative of various utopian writers whose works reflect, in a positive or negative way, their assessments of technology. Shelley's scientist, Dr. Frankenstein, created a monster which proved uncontrollable, but the monster was made of flesh and blood. Later man felt threatened by his relation to the machine and believed that the significance of his life was diminished by its needs. To us, the industrial machines of the last century seem relatively unsophisticated. In the twentieth century, the technological apparatus, the external symbols and signs of technology, have changed. Familiar to all of us are early films which depict the single-minded and increasingly daring scientist creating death rays and tinkering with brain transplants in a lab filled with strange apparatus. Later, the mad scientist faded into the eccentric and harmless zany-professor version in the Disney films. Death rays were replaced by super-elastic sneakers which allow the local basketball team to overcome its rivals. Today the scientist-technician is neither hero nor villain; superhuman hardware stands in his stead. In the recent film, *2001: A Space Odyssey*, the name of the computer is HAL; the human technicians in the film are nameless.

Twentieth Century Dystopias

If a technological utopia is a projection of the ideal possibilities inherent in technological advances, then the achievement of "utopia" seems closer to us than ever before. Scientific and technological advances in medicine and psychopharmacology seem to edge us closer to the elimination of physical and mental suffering; agricultural advances coupled with the control of the birth rate seem to edge us toward the elimination of want and the struggle for subsistence; communications satellites and other advances seem to put us closer to world-wide community and a better understanding of all races and cultures on the globe; even man's age-old dream of immortality no longer seems completely out of the question with the advent of organ transplants, cryogenics, and the replacement of human organs with artificial devices. These goals seem to be at least a part of the traditional meaning of "utopia."

Yet the saying "One man's utopia is another man's dystopia" is as true today as it ever was. Twentieth century utopias also tend to be twentieth century dystopias. Dystopian writers seem to see totally different meanings in the technological possibilities. The absence of suffering could mean a drug-induced

comatose existence; the absence of want, the elimination of all
strong desire in a blandly hedonistic Brave New World; the
global community, a monolithic technocratic world-state like
Orwell's *1984*; the absence of death, an eternally monotonous
existence of a "man" who is but a mutation of himself, a
symbiosis of man-machine-computer. Twentieth century dystopias are predominantly extrapolations of what the writers
feel are the destructive and dehumanizing effects of technology
and technological change. What follows are some of the dominant themes in dystopian writing. The list and illustrations are
by no means exhaustive of dystopian writings or dystopian
themes in this century.

The Destruction and Transmutation of Nature

When put in historical sequence, man's discovery and use of
diverse sources of power is instructive: the power of muscle,
water, wind, steam, electricity, the atom and solar power. The
last four sources of power came into use only in the last 300
years of man's history. The explosion of a nuclear device over
Hiroshima meant something more than the end of the war for
Japan. It meant a power available to man which far exceeded
anything he had previously known. Today nuclear energy may
save us all from the complete exhaustion of our energy resources. It also means the possibility of a cataclysmic explosion which would destroy the earth. One of the best known
dystopian novels in the 1950's, which grew out of this possibility, is Nevil Shute's *On the Beach* (1957), which depicts the
aftermath of a nuclear explosion that gradually wiped out life
on earth and presented the temporary survivors on a sub-
marine with some horrible choices in their few remaining hours.
The reader gets the impression that judgment day has come, but
the task, traditionally reserved for God, has been performed by
man. Several films, such as *The Beast from 20,000 Fathoms*
and the Godzilla series, also developed the horrible future effects of nuclear explosion and fall out: total destruction or
grotesque monsters from the deep, beyond anything Dr. Frankenstein imagined.

The theme of the tinkering biologist, experimenting with his
atomic-energy life rays and synthetic nutrients made possible

by man's new power, caused the size of nature to be scaled up and down in films: miniaturized man in a normal-sized world battled ants and spiders; giant grasshoppers, flies and insects threatened to take over the world. Ironically, the world was usually saved by man's superior intelligence and the fire power made possible by his new technology. Yet running through these dystopian visions of the destruction and transmutation of nature was often a Promethean theme: the new knowledge and the power it brings represent an act of rebellion which goes beyond the order of things. "There are some things man should not know."[6]

Manipulated Man

For many, technology not only threatens man's physical environment, it also encroaches upon his inner life and freedom. Dystopian writers see in recent work done in fields such as behavioral psychology, biogenetics, psychopharmacology and psychosurgery the possibility of a completely conditioned human being, devoid of freedom and individuality. A recent science-fiction novel by Michael Crichton (author of *The Andromeda Strain*) entitled *The Terminal Man* depicts a computer scientist who, because of illness, undergoes psycho-surgery. After the operation, his brain is controlled by an electroneurological device connected to a stamp-size computer implanted in his neck. In the novel, the "terminal" man's consciousness is likened to a television screen which merely "reads out" the electronic input. Genetic manipulation and psychological conditioning through drugs and propaganda are also a central theme of the classic dystopia, Aldous Huxley's *Brave New World*. The number and kind of children that should be produced are determined by the state engineers in the lab; the lab also produces the SOMA pills which are the source of the pacified smug happiness of the citizens. The efforts of "The Savage" to heroically revolt from this drug-conditioned nightmare are doomed to failure. More recently, psychological conditioning is a central theme in Stanley Kubrick's film of Anthony Burgess' *A Clockwork Orange* (written in 1962). The defiant and violent teenager, Alex, is "cured" of his violence by the clever use of biochemical and behavioral therapies. When the pacified Alex attempts suicide, the State regards its methods unsuccessful. Alex is then "unconditioned" and returns to his old ways.

Manipulated Society

We now possess almost all the technological advances suggested by Bacon in his utopia and are virtually able, in his words, "to effect all things possible." Cryogenics studies the behavior and preservation of bodies in extremely low temperature environments; we have high towers to study the weather and also orbiting satellites; we can desalinate salt water; we can create all sorts of artificial metals; and napalm will fit his description of "wildfires burning in water." But in his utopia Bacon also proposed that science and technology be associated with political power—that technicians (Salomon's House) be the rulers of the *New Atlantis*. One of the contemporary dystopian themes expresses the fear that this is precisely what is happening in modern society and that direct control of the societies of the future will be in the hands of an elite of scientist-technicians who will rule by their own norms of efficiency and production.

Again, the projection of this dire vision by dystopians is based upon some evidence in fact. In the United States, scientific and technological experts have been playing an increasing role in the councils of political power. Our immense, complex governmental structure relies considerably on technology in, for example, its military actions, its assessment of military and economic strategies, and its technical assistance programs. But the dependence is mutual. Major scientific and technological developments, either within or without our universities, require enormous funding and collective effort (such as our space program). Given this increasing interdependence, the dystopians project the growth of an elitist technological managerialism which could assume control of every aspect of society, centralize the sophisticated decision making process in the society, and create a technocracy which is completely inimical to the ideals of a participatory democracy.[7]

Many dystopian writers who focus on this theme of a manipulated society move toward the genre of social criticism. Zamiatin's early science-fiction novel *We* (1920) is an indictment of a dehumanized Soviet society early in this century, and technology plays a large part in the means used for dominance. The author's projected society is completely isolated in an artificial environment; in the name of efficiency, numbers replace personal names, and all aspects of the individual's life and social relations are regulated by the State, the omnipotent Benefactor. Zamiatin's work influenced George Orwell's classic presentation of a manipulated society, *1984*, dominated by Big Brother who controls the society under one discipline; feeling and emotion are repressed; privacy is illicit and made impossible by the ubiquity of eavesdropping devices.[8]

To complete this quick scan of jeremiads about technology, we should at least mention an area of dystopian literature which more clearly merges into political and social criticism. For these writers, technology represents the total condition of modern man in the West, a world-view, a set of values and a way of thinking which has its roots in the very beginnings of western civilization. Moreover, these writers feel that the techno-scientific world-view has eroded other modes of thinking and life styles and has demythologized man's world in order to make it technologically manageable. Technology is mistrusted because the values which both created technology and are fostered by it are exclusive of all other values.

Two well-known writers who interpret technology along these lines are Herbert Marcuse and Theodore Roszak. Because they see the scientific world view as exclusive and closed to other perspectives and its impact essentially destructive of human values, the amelioration of technological change is not enough. They call for a radical change in man's view of himself and the world, an emancipation from the logic of dominance implicit in scientific rationality and the canons of behaviorism and operationalism. Marcuse's *One Dimensional Man* points to the tensions between science and life in Freudian and Marxian terms. Scientific rationality, which Marcuse interprets as an ideology, limits the scope of man's sublimation and creates an irreconcilable tension with the needs and wants of people. While Marcuse calls for a less repressive society, his dystopian projection is a totally one-dimensional society—a society whose members have their needs and desires uniformly determined by the technological apparatus and the vested interests which control it. In *The Making of a Counter Culture*, Roszak calls for a transformation of man's consciousness and a rejection of "the myth of objective consciousness" which he feels lies at the heart of man's alienation and stifles his imagination and feeling. He sees the rejection of scientific perspectives and modern technology on the part of many in the "counter culture" as the seeds for a return to man's awareness of the significance of the mystical and transcendent. The ubiquitous technocracy can be undone only by the new consciousness present in the various movements of the counter-culture.

Utopian Thought and Modern Technological Society

Utopian writers project an ideal life in an ideal society; dystopian writers project a hellish life in a hellish society. In both cases they may be only fantasies. But a history of such projections indicates thay they are far from being merely fanciful. They are both responses to and extrapolations from the changing, conflicting realities and possibilities inherent in the history of a period. As we have indicated, technology has not only been an important factor in social change, it has continually redefined the possibilities and choices open to man. Partly because of these new possibilities, traditional utopian literature seems curiously irrelevant to our times. Two prevalent forms of literary utopia have been the retrospective utopia, which looked longingly back to a golden age, and the "island utopias," which chose some contemporary but spatially remote place upon which to project man's visions. The possibility of a return to a golden age, to a celebration of Rousseau's primitive savage, seems now out of the question. Our technological civilization seems completely discontinuous with our past. Our experience seems so discrete, so without precedent, that our imagination can get to the past only by means of the time machine of H. G. Wells or by the complete nuclear destruction of all of civilization. Likewise, the earth seems exhausted of completely isolated islands. Modern utopian/dystopian writers have increasingly emphasized that if heaven or hell is to come to us, it must come to all of us, it must be global or world-wide in scope. But of course space technology has opened up other places for us. Our imagination can easily move on to other islands in space.

Technological change has not only cut us off from the past and moved us out into space; the pace and magnitude of change have also brought the future closer to us. Forecasters armed with computers and computer simulation models are an essential part of big business and government. Yet the pace of change also makes our future uneasy. We have a deepened awareness of the seeming irrationalities of the present with its warfare and starvation amid plenty and its clash of new technologies with traditional institutions and values. There seems to be no stable context in the present from which we can create a whole vision necessary for a utopian projection. We have "future shock," our realities do outstrip our vision, and we seem only able to extrapolate our dreams and nightmares from the threads of uncertain trends and shaky evidence.

Both the complexities and the unanticipated consequences of technological change have brought to the fore the need to develop possibilities into probabilities. Social planning has been of major significance to the utopian writer, but traditionally his planning has had its justification in his ethical and normative philosophy, his conceptions of social justice, human happiness, and the ends of human life. If our description of technology and utopia/dystopia was essentially correct, the early days of modern history represent a glad acceptance of technology and a naive assessment of the human and social cost of technological change. Much of twentieth century dystopian literature represents a rejection of technology and a naive assessment of the human and social costs of that rejection. Although utopian/dystopian literature has raised the normative questions, it has failed to supply us with the real means for social change. From the utopians, we too often get merely the promise of a vitamin-fortified, technological cornucopia; from the dystopians, we too often get the futile visions of a "Chicken Little." Technology has provided abundant means for social change but has not pressed for answers to the important normative questions asked by the utopians/dystopians. Indeed, in the name of science and technology, some have not only despaired of ever getting answers, they have rejected normative questions as unauthorized by the canons of science.

NOTES

1. Michael Harrington, *The Accidental Century* (Baltimore: Penguin Books, Inc., 1965), p. 16. Harrington deplores the haphazard way in which technology is introduced into our society. One of his major points is that, for too long a time, technological change has been introduced solely in the interest of private purpose and gain.

2. In our day, government support of science and technology is extensive. Federal support of scientific research and development has recently reached as high as $17 billion annually. That the emphasis is on the utilitarian, short-range payoff is indicated by the fact that only $2.6 billion of this money was earmarked for basic research. The recent completion of the Apollo series and the cost of the war in Vietnam have diminished the percentage of the Federal budget going into science and technology.

3. After several years and many re-written constitutions, the experiment failed miserably. Owen was also important to the early stages of the labor movement. See Peyton E. Richter (ed.), *Utopias: Social Ideals and Communal Experiments* (Boston: Holbrook Press, Inc., 1971), pp. 98ff.

4. This theme of "the machine-take over" is portrayed in Kurt Vonnegut's novel *Player Piano* (1967). In Vonnegut's novel, man tries to revolt against his automated machine-run world. Unlike Butler's Erewhonians, the attempted reversion to a previous state of society with man in control is put down by the machines.

5. Morris' rejection of technology can be compared with a more recent novel, *Islandia* (1942), by A. T. Wright. Wright depicts a society at the South Pole which is confronted with all the so-called benefits of technology. The islanders reject most of them because of the cost they would have to the social and political values they already enjoy.

6. Rachel Carson and others have reminded us of a quieter, slower catastrophe: the long-range ecological consequences of our technology, the cumulative effects of chemicals and atomic waste upon our fragile spaceship earth. However, in his recent book, *The Doomsday Syndrome* (New York: McGraw-Hill, 1972), John Maddox rightly warns us that the preoccupation with the threat of distant ecological doom may distract us from doing something now about our environment.

7. Many of our universities have recognized the important issues which arise from technology in a democracy. A few programs in "Science, Technology, and Public Policy" have been started at universities across the country.

8. The theme of "no place to hide" is prevalent in films today. Scenes in films such as *Seven Days in May* and *Doctor Strangelove* are filled with wiretaps, television cameras, computerized data banks, pocket cameras, and tape recording devices. For a serious discussion of the impact of physical and psychological surveillance devices, see Alan F. Westin, *Privacy and Freedom* (New York: Atheneum, 1971) and Arthur P. Miller, *The Assault on Privacy: Computers, Data Banks, and Dossiers* (Ann Arbor: University of Michigan Press, 1971).

9. For an alternative view which asserts that our contemporary technological society is not anywhere near this monolithic, see Victor Ferkiss' *Technological Man: the Myth and the Reality* (New York: New American Library, 1969). See especially chapter 8, "Technological Change and Cultural Lag."

Marxism and Utopia
PAVEL KOVALY

"Every revolutionary ends by becoming either an oppressor or a heretic."
Albert Camus, *The Rebel*

"In the communist society," Peter said, "people will not be subordinated and enslaved by the division of labor, since the contradictions between mental and physical labor will have vanished."

"And," Joe added, "labor will no longer be a means of livelihood but it will become life's principal need and, after all, the productive forces will increase and there will be an abundance of everything."

"Then it will be possible to realize the dictum," Peter continued, "from each according to his ability, to each according to his needs."

"All that you are talking about," Charles objected, "can never be accomplished. It is an impossible utopia. Look how it works in Russia and China."

"But," Peter remarked, "we live under different conditions. Our society is an highly industrialized society, it cannot be compared with the development in the countries mentioned and

Pavel Kovaly is Associate Professor of Philosophy at Northeastern University and a frequent contributor to *Studies in Soviet Thought*.

therefore also the results will be different. In the future society, all alienation of man will disappear, the State will wither away and a new man will emerge."

The Marxist Critique of Utopianism

There are people who criticize Marxism and its vision of the future society as utopian. The Marxists refute such argument, admitting only occasionally some utopian features in Marxism, and maintain that Marxist theory is based on scientifically discovered laws of social development. Therefore, they argue, it is on the whole anti-utopian. The view I venture to propose is that Marxism is both anti-utopian and utopian. It depends on how utopia is conceived and from what standpoint it is considered.

Those who characterize Marxism as a utopian theory point chiefly to Marx's vision of the future socialist and communist society. They argue that the founders of Marxism critically examined negative features of the capitalist society during the period of the first industrialization, and in their moral fervor suggested a utopian organization in which society would take overall responsibility for the well-being and happiness of all its members. The future communist society becomes thus a utopia comparable with many other utopias in the history of Western thought, such as those suggested by Plato, Francis Bacon, Thomas More, Campanella, Morelly, Mably, Saint-Simon, Fourier, Owen and others. This argument puts Marxist theory about the future society on the same plane with the other visions of the ideal organization of society. Nevertheless—and in this sense the contention of the Marxists is quite correct—Marxist considerations about the future communist society differ considerably from all other social utopias.

Marxist philosophy began as an attempt to construct a philosophic world-view that would embrace general human knowledge and give clear answers to major philosophic and social problems. It was meant to be a theory for understanding the major laws of nature, society, and human thinking. Apart from the philosophy of nature, it critically examined the existing state of social relations and suggested ways of changing them. As a result of this radical criticism of the capitalist social order, Marx and Engels reached the conclusion that society would

necessarily undergo radical changes which would bring about
the socialist revolution, the dictatorship of the proletariat,
socialism and communism.

Marxist philosophy had been created in sharp opposition
to all previous utopian visions of the future social organization.
Its founders claimed that they had discovered the real motive
forces of the history and development of society. They were
found in the conflict between the social character of labor and
the individual private ownership of the means of production.
There exists an antagonism, Marx and Engels maintained,
between those who own the means of production and use them
for exploitation, and the others who do not own them and are
exploited. The class struggle between the capitalists and the
proletariat resulting from this antagonism would grow, and
eventually, they predicted, would be resolved in the socialist
revolution by the abolition of the private ownership of the
means of production. If the majority of people led by the proletariat and its Communist parties were to recognize this major
motive force of history, they would acknowledge it and work
and fight for the accomplishment of the revolution and the
construction of the new social organization.

From its very beginning Marxist social theory had been
marked by a critical attitude toward all previous utopian visions
of the future society. Friedrich Engels devoted a whole book to
the critical examination of Fourier, Saint-Simon and Robert
Owen, whom he called utopian socialists.[1] Engels does not
reject all their ideas. Some of their views he considers valuable.
For example, Engels agrees with Saint-Simon on the significance
of the proletariat and respects the fact that he considers politics
to be the science of production and economic condition to be the
basis of social and political institutions. Engels also appreci-
ates Fourier's criticism of existing social conditions, and Owen's
proposals for a systematic refusal of class distinctions.

But Engels criticizes a number of the social theories of the
utopian socialists as incorrect. All three of them, he argues, have
one thing in common. They all underestimate the role of the
proletarian class, and not one of them appears to be a representative of the proletariat. They do not want to emancipate a particular class but to free all humanity at once and bring it into the
kingdom of reason and justice. They hope that some genius will

understand the truth about social development and introduce it
into social relations. For them, society presents nothing but
wrongs, and they consider it the task of human reason to remove them. They seek a new social system which will be imposed upon society by propaganda. These ideas are, in Engels'
views, fantastic.

The Marxist Analysis of Social Orders

Therefore, the founders of Marxism took upon themselves the
task of searching for the laws and motive forces of the historical
development of mankind. They thought they had found them in
the economic basis of society and in the conflict of opposing
social classes. The class struggle theory forms the basis of their
historical materialism. According to it, five social orders can be
discerned in the history of mankind: primitive communism, slave
social order, feudalism, capitalist society and communism (with
socialism being its first phase).

The major characteristic of primitive communism is the communist ownership of the primitive means of production (e.g.
tools, land) and the communist distribution of the results of
human labor. All other social orders are characterized by opposing social classes. In the slave social order there are two opposing
social classes: slave owners and slaves; in feudalism, feudal
lords and those who work on their land.

At the beginning of industrial development during the late
Middle Ages, two new social groups developed, the bourgeoisie
and the proletariat, which formed the main classes of the
capitalist social order. The major feature of capitalism is the
opposition between those who own the means of production and
those who do not own them. Marx and Engels envisaged a rapid
growth of industrial development and with it the continuous
sharpening of the conflict between capitalists and proletarians.
The proletarians not only would not own the means of production, but would continue to be impoverished and exploited
by the proprietors. They would not be paid the full value of
their labor but only a small part of it, and the capitalists would
own all the surplus value. Marx and Engels predicted that therefore the conflict between the capitalists and the proletarians
would sharpen and could only be resolved by the abolition of

the private ownership of the means of production and all exploitation of man by man. The founders of Marxism saw in this development the law of history.

According to the theory of historical materialism, all proletarians and their allies are called on to fight the capitalist social system, abolish the private ownership of the means of production, take them over in the socialist revolution, and introduce the dictatorship of the proletariat. During the dictatorship of the proletariat the proletarian class will hold all power over the whole society. Although Marx and Engels did not specify the length of it, they thought it would be a relatively short historical period. During this time, all private ownership of the means of production would be abolished along with conflicting classes and exploitation of man by man. Socialism, the first phase of the communist social order, would be constructed. In it all means of production and distribution would be socialized; all spheres of social life would be ruled by reason; man would become the master of nature and of social development, overcoming the alienation and dehumanization caused by capitalism.

The Marxist Future Society

Marx did not describe the details of the new future order, but suggested a few general conditions essential to the transformation of society by the socialist revolution. Apart from the abolition of the private ownership of the means of production, the major conditions were: abolition of property in land, introduction of a graduated income tax, abolition of all rights of inheritance, confiscation of property of all emigrants and rebels, centralization of credits by the State and exclusive monopoly of the State, centralization of the means of communication and transportation by the State, and centralized State economic planning.[2]

Marx presupposed that the socialist revolution would introduce a society in which the free development of each person would be the condition for the free development of all. In communism the antithesis between mental and physical labor would vanish, the productive forces would increase, conditions for the development of the individual would be created, and the communist dictum would at last be realized: "From each according to his ability, to each according to his needs!"[3]

When outlining the general conditions of the future society, Marx and Engels endowed the proletariat with a mission to be the leading class in the socialist revolution. The proletariat was to use its political power and supremacy to abolish the private ownership of the means of production and to centralize them in the hands of the State, which was supposed to represent the proletariat organized into the ruling social class. They saw in the centralized society the chief form of rational social organization. Central economic planning was to be the major tool in the realization of the future utopia. In achieving their goal, they clearly and openly admitted that "despotic inroads on the rights of property and on conditions of the bourgeois production" would be unavoidable.[4]

Marx and Engels drew their conclusions about the historical development of mankind from existing social facts and conflicts. But they generalized and absolutized them into major motive forces of social development. On the basis of one aspect of social conflict they formed a social theory, thus changing partial phenomena into an overall explanatory schema. Similarly, they based their general views about the future society on their examination of wrongs and conflicts during the industrial revolution. In the period of the industrial revolution, especially in England in the first half of the nineteenth century, Marx saw the linear growth of the industrial proletariat, along with its impoverishment. On this basis he made a project that the working class would grow constantly in numbers, social conflict would sharpen, and the first step in the future socialist revolution would occur as the proletariat was raised into the position of the ruling class. But the actual subsequent development of the industrialized countries considerably modified the conditions that formed the presuppositions of Marx's theory. To mention just a few examples, neither the number of proletarians nor the exploitation grew as Marx presupposed. Powerful labor movements developed during the nineteenth century, and during the twentieth century the linear growth of the proletariat and its impoverishment have changed entirely. Rapid industrialization during the post-industrial era did not intensify the impoverishment of the working class. The introduction of modern scientific inventions, complex mechanization, and automation, reversed the process of the growth of the working class. In the future, as contemporary projections show, the number of workers in the most industrialized countries will diminish, rather than grow.

The subsequent development of Marxism took over Marx's critical method and his long-term projections. But it soon became evident that Marx's criticism had been only partial, and the correctness of it gradually diminished. Since the social realities and facts of the industrial world confirmed less and less Marx's original theories, the utopian and messianic elements of his vision were more and more generalized and absolutized, becoming articles of faith. As it was impossible to prove Marx's vision of the future, it began to function as a guideline for those Marxists who believed in it. The method of criticism turned into a belief in the future social order, and from here stems the messianic and utopian character of the entire Marxist teaching.

For a long time, the Marxists stressed the necessity of social development leading toward the socialist revolution and the dictatorship of the proletariat. That the march of history toward communism was governed by iron social laws has been the most important feature of the Stalinist version of Marxism. It put economic determinism into the roots of all human activities. Stalinism has abolished individual man in theory, and has always been willing to sacrifice individuals so long as this contributes to the salvation of the socialist revolution.

Marx on Alienation

Today we can observe a considerable reaction among some Marxists against Stalinism. This varies in both content and form, but its main feature is the return to the works of the young Marx, especially his *Economic and Philosophic Manuscripts*. Marx's views set forth there on man, alienation and de-alienation have become the source of many new studies in social theory, among both Marxists and non-Marxists. Significantly, it is in these parts of Marx's works that the messianic and utopian features of his thought are probably stronger than anywhere else. Let us follow his critical analysis of the alienation of man under capitalism and consider his suggestions for overcoming it in order to reveal its utopian character and practical effects.

Marx traces the origin of human alienation to the private ownership of the means of production. Alienation, according to his theory, is an economic and social problem related to the products of man's labor, concerned with man as a social being and with the relation of the individual and society. In alienated relations man's products acquire an independent and autonomous existence. They turn against man and subordinate him; man is unable to control them. Not only man's products (e.g. goods on the market) become alienated from him; so also do his social relationships (e.g. political parties and the State). Marx further describes self-alienation in which man is alienated from his own self. This also is rooted in the economic alienation in the capitalist society. Let us follow in detail particular features of Marx's analysis of alienation of man under capitalism, as they form the basis of his utopia.

All men express themselves, produce or create. They objectify themselves in labor, productive activity or creation. In capitalism their objectifications are estranged from those men who produce or create them. All products of human labor are thus estranged, alienated from their immediate producers, and they lead an independent existence on the market.

But not only are the products of man's labor alienated from man. Human labor, man's productive activity, is alienated from the worker. In the capitalist society, Marx argues, the labor of a worker does not belong to him. He has to sell it on the market. His labor is alienated from him and belongs to someone else. In the process of the estrangement from labor man looses his unique characteristics and his humanity.

"What constitutes the alienation of labor?", Marx asks. His answer is that the work becomes external to the worker, not part of his nature through which he fulfills himself but something which leaves him with feelings of misery, self-rejection and exhaustion rather than well-being and contentment. "The worker, therefore, feels himself at home only during his leisure time, whereas at work he feels homeless." Work is something external to himself, something he does not do for himself but for somebody else. "In fact, in work he does not belong to himself but to another person."[5]

The worker's own activity becomes alien to him, independent from him, and does not belong to him. "This is self-alienation."[6]

In it man is alienated from his humanity, from the possibility of free, spontaneous activity; he alienates himself, loses himself, is objectified, fragmented, crippled and dehumanized. He is estranged from himself, from his essence; he becomes a self-alienated being. And since all these characteristics apply to all men, they lead to the alienation of an individual from others and of others from an individual.

In considering alienated social relations, Marx examines the State. Originally created and controlled by men, the State in a capitalist society eludes the control of people and starts to function as an autonomous social force, independent of the majority of people. It develops into an organization which is not subordinated to the majority of people, but rather individuals are subordinated to it. And the greater the alienation of the State from man, the more it becomes the tool of the capitalist class, turns against man, exerts more and more oppression against the individual, becomes a subject of social development and changes its members to manipulated objects.

Marx's explanation of alienation was based on partial phenomena existing in the capitalist society, especially during the period of industrialization. But he generalizes them and at the same time reduces their source to the economic factors, the ownership of the means of production. And since he makes a direct linear relationship between private ownership and alienation, and absolutizes it into a major evil, it is not surprising that he makes its linear negation the basis of his messianic utopia and sees the overcoming of alienation in the abolition of the private ownership of the means of production. Marx thus views communism as "the positive abolition of the private property, of human self-alienation." It is "the real appropriation of human nature through and for man," and "the return of man to himself as a social, i.e. really human being. . . ."[7]

It could be argued that Marx sees the realization of his utopian views on de-alienation of man in the distant communist future. But his utopia makes the overcoming of alienation directly dependent upon the abolition of private property. His argument has enabled some contemporary Marxists in the Soviet Union to argue that since in the Soviet society the private ownership of the means of production had been abolished in the socialist revolution, the alienation of man does not exist there

any more. And Marx gives more than one reason to support
this argument since he expresses his utopian views quite clearly
when he directly relates private property to alienation and the
abolition of the private property to de-alienation. "The positive
supercession of private property," Marx states, "is, therefore,
the positive supercession of all alienation."[8]

For the new future society Marx also envisions the advent of
a new, utopian man. As against the real man of the bourgeois
society, he holds up the ideal of the well-rounded, complete,
true man. In contrast to the alienated man, the man in his utopia will be the whole, universal man. Since Marx predicts the
end of the division of labor and the substitution of a frequently
changed "freely chosen human activity" for labor, he sees a
member of his utopian society as a man who can fully realize
all the possibilities that make up his human essence. Universal
man will be man freed of all alienation.

In some recent Marxist works the problem of alienation and
the overcoming of it is explained together with a vision of a
universal, total, true man. Such authors maintain that the
socialist revolution represents an act of human self-emancipa-
tion, and it is only in communism that man will be liberated from
all alienation and will fully develop his personality. These
theories postpone the overcoming of alienation of man to the
future communist society. In theory, communism, not socialism,
is seen as an organization in which all alienation will be abolished, and a full, unrestricted, non-alienated development of
personality made possibly.

Alienation in Theory and Practice

Let us now consider the effects of Marx's utopian views both
in theory and in practice. According to them, the socialist
revolution should expropriate private property and make it the
property of all people represented by the State. Does the alienation of man in the described forms disappear with the socialist
revolution or not? If it does, Marx's theory is correct; if it does
not, Marx's theory is historically limited and partial, and consequently, its basic presuppositions are incorrect.

The socialist revolution has been accomplished in a number
of states. Has the alienation of man disappeared there as Marx

presupposed it would? For a long time, the prototype of socialism has been Stalinism and Neo-Stalinism in the Soviet Union. Many people today think that Stalinism as a social system is characterized by oppression, purges, persecution of political opposition, show-trials, labor camps and mass executions. But all these features, though often present, do not form the very essence of Stalinism. There is a major cause that accounts for all these disastrous features. It is the enormous concentration of social and political power in the hands of the leadership of the Communist Party and ultimately in the hands of one person, Stalin, during the period of his reign, and in the hands of a few people in the contemporary Neo-Stalinist period. The exercise of absolute control over all spheres of human life was the essence of Stalin's attempt to bring about the realization of Marx's utopia.

We saw that according to Marx's theory the primary factor of alienation in capitalism is that the product of human labor is being taken away from the immediate producer and put on the market. In the socialist society, the means of production are owned and run by the State and the State is run by one ruling party. Socialist revolution with its expropriation of private property does not remove the fact that products of human labor are taken away from the immediate producer and put on the market. On the contrary, it not only alienates the results of human labor from their immediate producers, but in addition dominates and governs both production and distribution. The market, including prices, is totally dominated by the State and ultimately by the Communist Party. Man is thus alienated not only from his immediate products but also from the market. Consequently, man is again alienated from his labor.

The socialist revolution was supposed to have abolished what Marx, following other economists, described as "surplus value." Briefly stated, this means that the worker is not paid the full value of his labor but only a part of it. The other part—the surplus value—is the property of the owner. But in the socialist society surplus value has continued to exist in another form and is appropriated, dominated and manipulated by the State. For that reason we can call the economic system of current Marxist socialist states State capitalism. Consequently, we can conclude that in such socialist states as the Soviet Union man's

labor does not belong to him; he has to sell it primarily to the
State and organizations dominated by the State. Thus his labor
belongs to someone else. By this process, man under socialism
becomes more and more alienated from his human essence, because his labor is manipulated by forces that do not depend on
him, that are external to him.

Since in socialism the products of human labor and labor itself are alienated from man by social forces that he cannot control, his free activity, his "species-life" becomes alienated as
well. Man makes his life-activity, his being, only a means for his
existence. The social sources of alienation of man in the socialist
society are in general deeper and stronger than in any other
social system, since both human labor and man's existence are
governed by social forces that are independent of him and totally
manipulate and rule his life, thoughts, feelings. Man is not free
to realize his own potentialities. His possibilities are strictly
limited and channeled, and his basic human rights and freedom
are either completely abolished or considerably restricted.

Finally, we could rephrase Marx's contention about the alienation of man from the others. A direct consequence of the various
forms of alienation—from the results of his labor, from his
labor itself, from life-activity, and from his species-life—is that
man under socialism is alienated from other men. All of these
forms of alienation affect not only one man but his relationships
to all men; consequently, man is alienated; he feels estranged
from his fellow human beings.

Furthermore, according to Marxist theory, the main alienated
social organization, the State, was supposed to wither away. By
the withering away of the State, Marx meant that all major
functions of the State would be taken over by all people. As a
separate organization the State was to fulfill only minor tasks
of administering things. All major social functions were to be
governed by all men rather than by a separate social and political organization. But this theory also proved to be a utopian
vision. In the socialist society the State has existed and continues to exist. For almost half a century, Stalin's theory of the
intensification of the class struggle has promoted the strength-
ening and bureaucratizing of the State in Marxist dominated
countries. Today no Marxist would continue to defend Marx's
view about the withering away of the State. Under socialism, the

State mechanism retains all its repressive tools, and the entire social life is centrally and hierarchically organized in order to control all spheres of human life—economic, social, political, scientific, artistic and ideological.

Contemporary Functions of the Marxist Utopia

We mentioned Marx's utopian vision of a universal man of a future society, who would emerge after the abolition of the private property, when the division of labor would disappear and "freely chosen human activity" would be substituted for labor as man proceeded to fully realize his human potentialities. All these ideas not only bear a clearly utopian character, sometimes attributed to "a youthful folly" of Karl Marx, but they can function as dangerous elements of a Marxian utopia, especially if a dictator believes in them and decides to impose them upon others by any means available.

A contemporary Polish Marxist philosopher, Adam Schaff, refers to Marx's views on the disappearance of the division of labor in the future society and on the universal man as "the naive whimsies of their young author,"[9] and suggests that alienation due to the inevitable division of labor can better be overcome by reducing working time. In his re-interpretation of Marx's theory of alienation, Schaff's final recommendation actually represents an admission of the improbable, utopian character of Marx's proposals for overcoming alienation under socialism, since he basically accepts the view which has been proposed for a long time by many non-Marxists (especially, by the Existentialists): "Alienation and its threats must be seen clearly and resisted consciously."[10] Concerning Marx's view of man in communism, Schaff remarks: "Reading the classic Marxist texts on man under communism one sometimes gets the feeling that they are utopian. No doubt they contain a residue of utopia."[11]

Thus the utopian features of Marxism are at last admitted by a Marxist. The explanation of how utopia functions in social and political life for the Marxists has yet to be given.

Social criticism and moral fervor might well have been the original motives of Marx and Engels when they inquired into social problems and outlined their vision of the future society.

The ideal end they portrayed might have seemed great, noble and just. But there are a number of reasons why their utopia has changed into its opposite.

First of all, the ideal end becomes the main or the only criterion of evaluating social movements and individual actions for the Marxist. All methods and means that are used are not judged from any ethical position but rather from the point of view of time and circumstances. All ethical values and moral standards are subjugated to the historical development toward the revolution and communism. This means that everything is judged from the point of view of history and the future. The glorious and magnificent goal, the communist utopia, justifies all means used for its attainment. Consequently, all actions and means which serve the goal become right, good, moral and just, no matter how immoral in other ethical perspectives they might be. All means are viewed and used with respect to this end. Accordingly, there are no moral and immoral acts; from the point of view of history, differences between right and wrong, ethical and unethical, vanish. There are only such acts or means which serve the goal and others which do not serve it. Those agents who perform acts which serve the end are moral, those who avoid it or refuse to serve the goal, become immoral. Marx's justification of the revolution and of the communist utopia is historical rather than ethical. And at all times it enables the use of immoral methods and means to reach the goal. The major constituents of Marx's utopia—communism, ideal justice, ideal freedom, universal man—not only justify immoral acts but virtually demand them. Violence, crime and terror are not only justified by the great goal to be attained but they become a virtue and the duty of an individual.

But the application of immoral methods and means, for no matter what purpose, necessarily changes the ideal vision, although originally it might have seemed noble. That is why the communist utopia bears a distinctly unethical, authoritarian and coercive character. That is why the socialist revolution in different countries of the contemporary world has introduced a social organization in which all economic and political power has become strictly centralized, absolutized and concentrated in the hands of one person or a few. Basic human rights have been abolished with the promise of ideal rights in the future; human freedom has been restricted or abolished under the pretext of complete human freedom under communism. Socialist revolution has introduced the reign of terror as necessary and justifiable in the transition to the new social order. The Marxist utopia presupposed the disappearance of the alienation of man and the emergence of a new man. But alienation has not been overcome; on the contrary, centralized society has brought about deeper social sources of alienation, since it has severely limited human choices, has curtailed freedom and has subjected and manipulated man. A new man has not emerged.

For more than half a century, this state of affairs has been maintained in the Soviet Union with the promise that basic human rights would be granted in the near future. But time and again the promise is postponed to the distant communist society. The communist utopian promise functions as a mystification of the present state of affairs and is used for its defense.

Another major reason why utopia has changed into its opposite is not external but concerns the inner attitude of man toward it. It asks man for a rational, voluntary, disciplined attachment. It demands that men join forces, actively working and fighting for the socialist revolution and communism. It not only justifies restrictions of freedom, but an individual is supposed to *accept* these restrictions, willingly and obediently subjecting his own self to them. In the name of a future ideal freedom it demands that man subordinate to it his rational capacities and very existence. Both in Marxist theory and in practice, freedom is usually conceived of as a willing, total, conscious submission of man's existence and thought to the communist movement. "The desire (for freedom)," the Marxist philosopher George Lukács writes, "must entail the renunciation of the individual freedom, it implies the conscious subordination of the self to that collective will that is destined to bring real freedom into being, and that today is earnestly taking first steps toward it. This conscious collective will is the Communist Party."[12] For Lukács, authentic freedom can be reached only through discipline and the unconditional absorption of the total personality in the practice of the movement.

Thus a utopian promise justifies not only external forces of oppression in social and political practice, but requires individual inner submission and subjection as well. Both from outside and in his inner life, a concrete living human being has been reduced to an object. The great, magnificent, utopian vision has turned man into a mere cog in the wheels of political apparatuses. Man has become negligible.

NOTES

1. Fourier, Charles, (1772-1837), French social philosopher. He projected a social utopia organized into small economic units (phalanxes) of 1620 persons. His doctrines spread to America. Brook Farm was for a time fourierist. The most successful community was the North American Phalanx at Red Bank, New Jersey.

Owen, Robert (1771-1859), British social reformer and socialist pioneer in the cooperative movement. A successful cotton manufacturer of New Lamark, Scotland, he constructed the community into a model industrial town, with nonprofitmaking stores, and, for the time, excellent working conditions. In 1828 he established the ill-fated community of New Harmony, Indiana.

Saint-Simon, Claude Henry de Rouvroy, comte de (1760-1825), French social philosopher, who advocated ideas that were supposed to do away with inequalities in property, distribution, and political power. His writings foreshadow socialism and European federation. His pupils constructed a system of "saint-simonism" calling for public control of the means of production.

2. See Karl Marx and Friedrich Engels, "The Communist Manifesto" in *The Marx-Engels Reader*, ed. by R. C. Tucker, (New York: W. W. Norton, 1972) p. 352-353.

3. K. Marx, "The Critique of the Gotha Program"; in *The Marx-Engels Reader*, Tucker, *op. cit.*, p. 378.

4. Marx and Engels, "The Communist Manifesto," *Ibid.*, p. 352.

5. Karl Marx, *Early Writings*, ed. by T. B. Bottomore, (New York: McGraw-Hill, 1963), p. 125.

6. *Ibid.*, p. 126.

7. *Ibid.*, p. 155.

8. *Ibid.*, p. 156.

9. Adam Schaff, *Marxism and the Human Individual*, (New York: McGraw-Hill, 1971), p. 135.

10. *Ibid.*, p. 138.

11. *Ibid.*, p. 175.

12. George Lukács, *History and Class Consciousness*, (Cambridge, Mass: MIT Press, 1971), p. 315.

Skinner and the Morality of
Melioration
MELVIN M. SCHUSTER

Various Responses to Skinner's Views

IN THE UTOPIAN NOVEL, *Walden Two*,[1] B. F. Skinner presents what he considers to be a reasonably attractive picture of a society run according to the techniques of behavioral psychology. It is harmonious, characterized by good will and fellowship, offering leisure and entertainment to its members but enough work to assure the well-being of the individual and the community; art is encouraged; education is innovative, painless, and relevant; and in general "people are truly happy, secure, productive, creative, and forward-looking."[2] Nonetheless, many have looked upon Skinner's world as destructive of the most valuable qualities of human existence. The reaction against him has, in fact, been so virulent and intense that Skinner recently remarked upon the "fanatical opposition," the "bitterness," and the "emotional instability" of his attackers.[3]

There are a number of reasons for the response other than

Melvin M. Schuster is Associate Professor of Social Science at Boston University, Division of General Education.

disagreement with Skinner's arguments. One is the uncom-
promisingly blunt manner in which he expresses his rejection
of sacred items such as freedom, responsibility, dignity. The
terms themselves are emotionally laden, and it could be expected
that a book with the title *Beyond Freedom and Dignity* would
arouse animosity and resistance even before being read. A
second source of irritation is the extension of Skinner's posi-
tivistic approach to areas where many moral issues are at stake,
where predictability is slight, the meaning of verification uncertain, and where care and caution are sometimes required to
keep ideology out of science. Finally, it is easy to misunder-
stand Skinner by confusing the two levels of analysis on which
he usually works: a here-and-now level of concrete action and
an abstract, theoretical level of explanation and justification.
Despite the connection of the two, they are still distinct, so that
what holds for one may not for the other, i.e., it is possible to
reject an idea on the level of application without rejecting the
explanation behind it, and vice versa. Skinner is quite open-
minded and flexible about such things. He tries to work with the
materials at hand, is aware of their limitation, of the possibility
of error, and is ready to make adjustments. His attitude, in short,
is experimental.[4]

The object of this paper is to sort out these complexities and
distractions in order to determine what can be said ethically
about the world that Skinner proposes. The study will move
through four areas: the ethical (his values), the metaphysical
(his determinism), the instrumental (his use of conditioning),
and the political (his elitism). It will begin, however, by placing
him within his proper context in social thought.

Skinner's Tradition

Skinner is part of a well-established tradition, extending from
the ancient to the modern world, which holds that the function
of political society is melioration, that is to say, the improvement
of man and the creation of the good life. This conception is
essential to Plato's *Republic*, of course, and serves in the
Gorgias as the standard in terms of which Socrates denies the
greatness of the reputedly great statemen of Athens.[5] Aristotle
gives expression to it when he claims that the state, "originating

in the bare needs of life," continues "in existence for the sake of the good life";[6] and Skinner continues in the same vein by reaffirming "the doctrine of human perfectibility"[7] and by having the fictional designer of Walden Two criticize our government for refusing to "accept the responsibility of building the sort of behavior needed for a happy state."[8] This tradition is understandably conducive to utopian thinking and to the idea of elitist rule, for if melioration is to have any significance at all, there must exist a good (in some sense), as well as an appropriate means for attaining it, and the good and its means must be knowable. With these ingredients it becomes possible to construct planned worlds of the Platonic or Skinnerian order, and it can then be argued—it seems impossible not to argue—that leadership and authority should reside in those people who possess the knowledge of means and ends required to bring the good life into being. Plato thought that his ideal society would always have to be governed by an intellectual elite because he believed that intelligence was inherited and few men were born with the intellectual potential to rule. Meliorists like Marx and Marcuse, on the other hand, with a strong humanistic bias, are rather optimistic about the possibilities of man. They consequently regard domination by the few as a transitional device needed to introduce the better world. Elitist rule, becoming unnecessary, is supposed to dissolve. Skinner inclines more toward Plato on this issue, despite his positivist orientation, for he would have rule by experts whose ranks are open to qualified citizens. While his conception of intelligence does not appear to have Plato's general biological rigidity, he does think that there will never be more than a small number of this "exceptional" type, and consequently never more than a few people to do the governing.[9]

It would seem from what has been said that the question concerning the nature of the good at which utopia aims would therefore be fundamental and occupy a central position in all melioristic social thought. Yet this is precisely the kind of question that Skinner condemns and associates with vacuous pedantry; he sees it as an irrelevant puzzle to be played with in university classrooms while the world outside buckles and bends under the problems of population, war, poverty, sickness, insecurity, and misery. Skinner directs his ire at those who are so

intellectually meticulous that they will do nothing until every bit
of knowledge is dusted and put neatly in its place. But whether
or not we know what The Good is, we can surely agree "that
health is better than illness, wisdom better than ignorance, love
better than hate, and productive energy better than neurotic
sloth."[10] A summary of Skinner's concrete utopian goals appears
at the end of his last book:

> ". . . a world in which people live together without quarreling,
> maintain themselves by producing the food, shelter, and clothing
> they need, enjoy themselves and contribute to the enjoyment of
> others in art, music, literature, and games, consume only a reason-
> able part of the resources of the world and add as little as possible
> to its pollution, bear no more children than can be raised decently,
> continue to explore the world around them and discover better
> ways of dealing with it, and come to know themselves accurately
> and, therefore, manage themselves effectively."[11]

Even with regard to these he is apparently undogmatic. He
speaks of an "experimental ethics" that would "profit from
experience,"[12] because errors are always possible, and what
worked at one time may not at another.[13] The test is whether
it works; the justification he seeks is not speculative but experimental."[14]

Skinner on Values

To measure workability, Skinner turns to the survival of the
culture, and in so doing, and despite his pragmatic drive, faces
the problem of ultimate values. Cultural survival does not always harmonize with personal goods, or with the goods of
others, but it is the good that Skinner has fixed upon since he
thinks it is implied by any attempt to design an entire culture.[15]
He offers no further justification of it because he does not believe that one exists.[16] If this is not a very philosophic attitude,
it is at least shared by a number of philosophers who also
speak of the indefensibility of first principles. At any rate, some
may refuse to accept the consequences of Skinner's position
since, for example, it would follow that brutality is wrong and
justice right merely because of their survival value and, in
general, that "those principles which are with us today have been

most valuable in this respect."[17] But such a rejection does not constitute grounds for a moral criticism of his utopia. There may be more to ethics than survival, but survival is surely not an unethical goal. Even John Locke's advocacy of natural rights is qualified by recognition of a "nobler cause" which is "the peace and preservation of all mankind."[18] The survival of mankind may ultimately prove to be in conflict with morality, yet in designing a community it is not unreasonable to proceed on the opposite assumption.

Moreoever, when Skinner argues that current values have achieved their status because they have had survival value, he is speculating. It is not the conclusion of an empirical science nor is it a philosophically substantiated position, but simply a reflection of his commitment to the survival of culture. In addition, he recognizes the difficulties of determining in advance whether any specific practice will have survival value.[19] One might ask for the survival value of eating with a fork, and innumerable other folkways. The point is not that Skinner is making the claim that every detail is ultimately explainable in terms of its direct contribution to survival, but that in practice—and this is to be stressed—Skinner's ultimate value has virtually no role to play. It lacks both theoretical force, since undefended, and practical force, since too far removed. Thus, in any significant sense, Skinner's morality is really the concrete here-and-now morality discussed earlier; and the experimental validity of those values is, as he argues, obvious to all. It would be "quibbling" to attempt to justify them,[20] as absurd as a "centipede trying to decide how to walk."[21] And presumably it would be just as quibbling and just as absurd to attempt to justify them in terms of ultimate survival value.

In summary, Skinner's goals are actually commonly accepted ones vaguely and almost arbitrarily tied to an ultimate good of cultural survival. The immediate values are hardly unethical, and the ultimate good, though of little functional significance, can itself reasonably be adopted by anyone in a position of social responsibility. Whatever might be unethical about Skinner's world must be located in the means, since it cannot be found in the ends. In fact, the greatest controversy about Skinner has centered upon his manipulation and conditioning of man.

Skinnerian Determinism

Man is free, it is objected, and it is unconscionable to subject him to the indignity of behavioral engineering. He is neither a pigeon nor a rat nor a machine, and should not be treated as such. At this point the charge that Skinner is an enemy of freedom must be viewed in two ways: (1) that Skinner destroys human freedom, and (2) that he treats men as if they were not free. Neither charge bothers Skinner, for he does not believe that there exists a human freedom to destroy or violate. Whenever we attribute freedom to human behavior we should in fact attribute ignorance of its causes to ourselves.[22] Now it must be understood that when Skinner speaks of determinism he does not mean some kind of metaphysically necessary connection between cause and effect that smacks of the occult. Although he does continue to use traditional causal language, the terms "cause" and "effect" refer to nothing more than events observed in regular conjunction.[23] To say, then, that an instance of behavior is caused by something else, that it is determined, produced, elicited, conditioned, compelled, or induced, is simply to say that there is a law-like or functional relation between it and some other event.

Metaphysical assertions about man's freedom consequently fall outside the domain in which Skinner works as a behaviorist. His science does give him, as it does other determinists, reason to question metaphysical freedom; but as a scientist, and without unwarranted extrapolation from simple observations of regularities, he is not in any position to make metaphysical claims about the nature of man or social reality. In fact, Skinner treats determinism as a first principle which is not one bit more capable of rational substantiation than is the ethical principle of cultural survival.[24] Not a morsel of reason or evidence is offered in support of his indefensibility thesis. Skinner seems to consider cultural survival as a kind of methodological principle for anyone involved in the utopian enterprise of culture-building. Determinism is again a methodological principle for him, since he believes it is his task as a scientist to seek the order contained within the subject matter, that is to say, its pattern and regularities. This is what he would term explanation, and it consists in discovering laws under which concrete cases are subsumed. Because it is also what Skinner calls determinism, it

follows that science, in assuming that regularities can be discovered, assumes the deterministic character of its subject matter;
and it follows, too, in the behavioral sciences, that every regu-
larity discovered is another instance of the determinism of man.

Libertarians get quite upset by this, though they need not,
because the fact that human behavior is regular does not entail
the conclusion that it is metaphysically determined. It would be
a strange kind of libertarianism that would argue for metaphysical freedom by insisting that a world of free men must be
characterized by irregularity, unpredictability, and sheer chaos.
On the contrary, rationality and human freedom have long been
associated, and if this is so, there is no reason for a libertarian
to be perturbed by the observation that free, rational beings
behave in orderly, predictable ways. Indeed, when a man is unpredictable it is often regarded as grounds for doubting his
rationality and for doubting that he is *in control of himself.*[25]

Furthermore, it is not clear that because freedom is valuable,
it is also fragile, as libertarians would imply. The existentialists
are perhaps to be admired for insisting that if there is freedom,
then there *is* freedom—a condition fundamental and unalterable,
a part of the nature of things, the way the world is.[26] Is it to be
destroyed by a touch of Skinnerian technique? Skinner's special
interest is in operant conditioning, a method based upon the fact
that when certain kinds of behavior are followed by certain kinds
of consequences, the likelihood of the behavior recurring increases. In these cases the consequences are termed reinforcers,
and the process of increasing the probability of behavior by
reinforcement is called operant conditioning. Now if human
freedom, metaphysically understood, could be destroyed by rewarding human acts, then Skinner would be right and the number of free acts, especially good ones, would be seriously de-
creased, or perhaps reduced to zero. But if not, the libertarian
would have no need to fear the use of operant conditioning.
Skinner does not claim to be the inventor of something which
never existed before; he claims, rather, to be speaking about
processes that have always characterized the way men act. Hence,
the problem is not really to determine whether men respond
to consequences, but whether in so doing they cease to be free.

Determinism carries ethical import only when it is interpreted
metaphysically, and it has been shown that Skinner denies,
and in fact has no basis for, interpreting it in that light. It

remains to be shown that conditioning destroys human freedom. Skinner never makes the claim that it does since he never admits freedom. Those who make the charge against him are therefore in the position of having to prove it, and that would be a sight—to see resolute defenders of the metaphysical freedom of man attempting to demonstrate that it can be crushed under the weight of reward. But it will be objected by Skinner's antagonists that if it is true that freedom cannot readily be annihilated, it is equally true that human beings are subject to a wide variety of influences upon their choice and behavior. The point is a truism and needs no great elaboration: men are influenced by the weather, by hunger and thirst, by economic rewards, by the opinion of others, by neighborhoods, schools, and the like. Let this influence principle, as it shall be termed, replace the determinist thesis. Skinner should have no objection, although he would undoubtedly want to say more. But it is enough for his purpose. Remember, he did not prove determinism, and he readily points out, first, that behaviorism is as yet incomplete, and, second, that the technology of behavior cannot determine every act and at best can only increase the likelihood of the recurrence of an act. Thus, seen in terms of what is, instead of what is claimed, Skinner's position appears to fall under the principle of influence rather than determinism.

Skinner lets himself be carried away when he asserts that "the hypothesis that man is not free is essential to the application of scientific method to the study of human behavior."[27] It may be true, as Frazier says in *Walden Two*, that "you can't have a science about a subject matter which hops capriciously about,"[28] but it is false to identify metaphysical freedom with capriciousness, as mentioned earlier. And the principle of influence gives sufficient stability to the subject matter to allow for probable recurrence and thus for intelligent application. This is not to say anything new or surprising or radical. Men have always known such things and they have sought to explain them, sometimes philosophically. What is radical and extreme is to maintain, as Skinner does, that there can be no science and no intelligent directing of behavior if there is an ounce of metaphysical freedom in the world. And what is equally radical and extreme is the view that if behavior is regular and capable of being influenced, it cannot be free.

Moral Criticisms of Skinner's Proposals

Given, then, Skinner's reasonable and morally praiseworthy immediate and concrete goals for man, and an apparently acceptable principle of influence, the question arises: what is morally wrong with Skinner's proposals? Is it not reasonable and right that mankind should use its available knowledge to control the environment and thereby cure, to the extent possible at the present stage of science, the innumerable and profound ills of the world? Is it not immoral to refuse? And is it not also reasonable, given the goals, to assign the task of achieving them to the people who know best how to do it—the scientist-experts? Skinner's utopian proposals represent an effort to systematize the possibilities for human growth by constructing a total environment wherein problems are resolved by rewarding the good but not the bad. That must be a significant characteristic of any conception of the good society. It is heaven without hell; it is that condition the absence of which accounts for the popular cynical meaning of such terms as "realistic" and "practical." Skinner may be over-optimistic about the possibilities for bringing utopia into existence, but it does not seem reasonable to condemn the vision as unethical.

Many of his critics would agree. As Chomsky says, Skinner's "libertarian and humanist opponents do not object to 'design of culture,' that is, to creating social forms that will be more conducive to the satisfaction of human needs, though they differ from Skinner in their intuitive perception of what these needs truly are."[29] But what are these needs as Skinner sees them? They are the concrete ones enumerated earlier, and it is hard indeed to imagine a humanist rejecting them. What seems really to be behind the criticism is the fear that Skinner's planned world would destroy the sensitivity, the spirit, and the intelligence of man. Skinner's man would be an automaton, a creature of habit. In reply, something should first be said about habit and rationality. Scientific and philosophic understanding of both appears to be deficient, for most human behavior is, in some sense of the word, habitual, although there are rational and irrational habits. It is surely incorrect narrowly to identify human rationality with the laborious, stumbling, sometimes cramped, deliberate process of thought that is often characteristic of the initial stage in learning. When a man once learns, he may act quickly and spontaneously. Should the learned, the wise, and the accomplished then be denied rationality, intelligence, spirit, and sensitivity, and these qualities be reserved for the fumbling child and the groping novice? The question of habit is obviously a moot point and cannot serve as an adequate basis for a moral criticism of Skinner.

Skinner wants to build rather than destroy intellect, aesthetic sensitivity, creativeness, and flexibility. People, he believes, should be taught how to think,[30] they should not be fed lies and propaganda,[31] and must not be personally stultified.[32]Skinner's educational ideas are directed to turning out a man who can face life with equanimity and confront the unexpected and the different without fear, but with intelligence and an open mind. Operant conditioning is the vehicle for accomplishing this. According to Skinner's understanding of cognitive thought, it, too, follows behavioral rules, so that by proper instruction employing behavioral techniques men's reasoning abilities will be expanded and made more efficient. One should not be upset by the use of the word "conditioning" in this context. As Skinner says, "No theory changes what it is a theory about."[33] What Skinner calls "conditioning," the humanist calls, and would continue to call, "learning" and "responding to reason."

Once the danger of determinism has been removed from conditioning, Skinner's method no longer constitutes a threat. And considering the goals he sets for it—the very reverse of what his critics fear—and his experimental attitude and willingness to change, the charge of mechanical man seems groundless. In fact, neither the ethical, the metaphysical, nor the instrumental areas have provided, upon reflection, a basis for a moral criticism of Skinner's social thought. There remains, then, the fourth and final area, the political.

Skinner and the Political Sphere

The charge against it is that Skinner's community is an authoritarian rather than a democratic one. But democratic communities may also be authoritarian (e.g., the tyranny of the majority), and it is not certain that the only legitimate political societies are democracies. Consider the virtues of Skinner's world:

it refuses to use the revolutionary and repressive techniques that meliorists like Marcuse support to bring about their better world;[34] membership is entirely voluntary, and even those who are born into it are free to leave; leadership is open to those with the interest and ability; respect is meted out to all and not simply to some on the basis of profession or political position; and people are not socially denounced or held in contempt for not being political activists.[35] Skinner believes that democracy is "almost certainly not the *final* form of government,"[36] and that today its goals can be better attained by using the elitist rule discussed earlier in the paper. But it must not be forgotten that Skinner's elitism, which is the basis of the political criticism, is a consequence of the meliorative hypothesis rather than of his behaviorism. It would be self-defeating to commit society to improvement and then to allow the incapable and the unable to take if from there. If an individual behaved in that way in his personal life, he would be accused of not really having the professed goal, or at least of having other goals that are more important. Plato's old argument has not lost its force and seems unavoidable for any meliorist: that if there is a standard and a commitment to its attainment, then the basis of political authority must be that special knowledge which enables the standard to be achieved. The meliorist hypothesis is humanistic but basically undemocratic.

Consider, further, the possibility of an election in Walden Two. Such a thing would not be,[37] but the people do vote in outside elections, and on those occasions they take the advice of the Political Manager and vote the straight "Walden Ticket" as they are told.[38] It is therefore reasonable to suppose that in such a voluntary community, if there were elections, the people would vote as the specialists direct—which would be to vote the specialists into their positions. The notion that the specialists should not give direction or advice would be absurd even in democracy, and it would be utterly destructive not only of Skinner's community but of the meliorative intent upon which it is based.

It must be borne in mind that Skinner's world is a people's world, a voluntary one, and as democratic as a meliorist political order can be. In fact, the community would avoid some of the abuses of which democratic societies are guilty.[39] But it is just

this popular, voluntary aspect of Walden Two that is upsetting
and that makes it appear dystopian even when it is meant to be
utopian. What seems wrong is not the fact that people try to
control the environment, improve their lives, influence one
another, use conditioning, employ one method of education instead of another, and refuse to punish. The only basis for an
ethical criticism is that adult people are being fashioned and
their lives molded in accordance with someone else's concept
of the good. It becomes more shocking as the control is centralized, massive, and efficient; and the more Skinner depicts its
accomplishments—which are significant—the worse it seems,
because the greater is its flaw. For people to be controlled
against their wills is an affront; but it is frightening and threat-
ening when the role of malleable material is voluntarily, even
eagerly adopted. Mill has said that society has no right to interfere in the life of the individual unless it is "to prevent harm to
others. His own good, either physical or moral, is not sufficient
warrant."[40] It is this classical, liberal principle that is violated
by Walden Two. And when an individual joins the community
voluntarily, he violates that responsibility which he has to
himself, to lead his own life and not submit to another, even
though that other were more competent and the life more com-
modious. It is the same point that Father Mapple makes in
Moby Dick: "Woe to him who would not be true, even though
to be false were salvation!"[41]

What is being suggested here is that the ethical criticisms of
Skinner are misplaced when they are directed against his goals,
or when they become needlessly embroiled in the issue of
determinism, or when they panic at the sound of the word "conditioning." The one moral flaw is its very foundation—the
meliorative hypothesis. The function of political society cannot
be the improvement of man and the creation of the good life; for
if it is, then there can be no moral objection to Skinner's world.

NOTES

1. B. F. Skinner, *Walden Two* (Paperback ed.; New York: The Macmillan Co.,
1962). This book will be identified in later references as *WT*.
2. These are Skinner's words in B. F. Skinner and Carl Rogers, "Some Issues
Concerning the Control of Human Behavior: A symposium," reprinted in
Humanistic Society, eds. John F. Glass and John R. Staude (Pacific Palisades,

Calif.: Goodyear Publishing Co., Inc., 1972), p. 333. This work will be identified in later references as *S and R*.

3. B. F. Skinner, *Beyond Freedom and Dignity* (New York: Alfred A. Knopf, 1972), p. 165. To be identified in later references as *BFD*.

4. The point is worth stressing. Skinner's experimental attitude is visable in all his writings. See, for example, *WT*, pp. 173-175; and *BFD*, 153-156.

5. Plato *Gorgias* 515A-517A.

6. *Politics* 1252b, 28-30. Benjamin Jowett's translation in *The Basic Works of Aristotle*, ed. Richard McKeon (New York: Random House, 1941).

7. B. F. Skinner, "Freedom and the Control of Man," reprinted in *Utopias*, ed. Peyton E. Richter (Boston: Holbrook Press, Inc., 1971), p. 289. This work will be identified in later references as *FCM*.

8. *WT*, p. 166.

9. *Ibid.*, p. 55.

10. *FCM*, p. 292.

11. *BFD*, p. 214.

12. *WT*, p. 174.

13. See *S and R*, p. 346; and *BFD*, pp. 175-176.

14. *WT*, p. 161. See, too, *BFD*, p. 153.

15. *BFD*, pp. 150, 182.

16. This point is made in *BFD*, p. 137 and *S and R*, p. 346. It also appears in B. F. Skinner, *Science and Human Behavior* (Paperback ed.; New York: The Free Press, 1965), p. 432. The latter book will henceforth be referred to as *SHB*.

17. *SHB*, p. 445.

18. *Second Treatise on Civil Government*, Chap. 2, Secs. 6, 7; in *Social Contract*, ed. Ernest Barker (New York: Oxford University Press, 1962), pp. 5, 6.

19. *SHB*, pp. 434, 436.

20. *FCM*, p. 292.

21. *WT*, p. 159.

22. See, for example, *FCM*, p. 293.

23. *BFD*, p. 7; *SHB*, pp. 23, 25.

24. *BFD*, p. 101; *WT*, p. 257.

25. On this subject, see E. R. Dodds' excellent book, *The Greeks and the Irrational* (Berkeley: University of California Press, 1968).

26. See, for example, Jean-Paul Sartre, *Existentialism*, trans. Bernard Frechtman (New York: Philosophical Library, 1947). Sartre uses such expressions as "complete freedom" (p. 55) to describe man's condition.

27. *SHB*, p. 447. See, too, *SHB*, p. 6 and *WT*, p. 256.

28. *WT*, p. 257.

29. Noam Chomsky, "The Case Against B. F. Skinner," *The New York Review of Books*, December 30, 1971, p. 24.

30. *WT*, pp. 119, 121.

31. *WT*, p. 207; *SHB*, p. 443.

32. *WT*, p. 209.

33. *BFD*, p. 213.

34. For Herbert Marcuse's views see, for example, "Ethics and Revolution," in *Ethics and Society*, ed. Richard T. De George (Garden City, N.Y.: Doubleday & Co., Inc., 1966), and "Repressive Tolerance," in Robert Paul Wolff, Barrington Moore, Jr., and Herbert Marcuse, *A Critique of Pure Tolerance* (Boston: Beacon Press, 1969). For Skinner's views on aversive measures, see his chapters on punishment in *BFD* and SHB. And for his observations on revolution see *WT*, pp. 195, 273.

35. *WT*, p. 167, and see, too, Chap. 8.

36. *FCM*, p. 294. Also, *WT*, p. 273.

37. *WT*, p. 267.
38. *Ibid.*, pp. 196-197.
39. *Ibid.*, pp. 268-269.
40. John Stuart Mill, *On Liberty* (New York: Appleton-Century-Crofts, Inc., 1947), p. 9.
41. Herman Melville, *Moby Dick* (New York: The Modern Library, 1950), p. 47.

Drugs and Utopia/Dystopia
WALTER H. CLARK

SEVERAL YEARS AGO in conducting a questionnaire study of the effects of psychedelic drugs, I had the opportunity to interview an 18 year old college freshman at one of the old line Eastern women's colleges. She had illegally ingested mescalin five or six times with a boy friend and was asked to rate the intensity of certain aspects of her drug experiences relative to the intensity of these same experiences in her normal life. Among the aspects to which she assigned the extreme rating of "beyond anything ever experienced or imagined" were a sense of the cosmic, a sense of unity and fellowship with people, joy, an esthetic experience with a heightened sense of color, music, and other aspects of beauty. Also beyond anything ever experienced or even imagined was the sense of learning, of growth and maturing, and the sense of the general significance of the drug sessions.

This was fairly typical of 100 users of the LSD-type chemicals surveyed, most of whom were in their twenties, the youngest of whom was 16, the oldest 48. Twenty users of cannabis

Walter H. Clark, Professor of Psychology of Religion, Retired, Andover-Newton School, is the author of *Chemical Ecstasy*.

drugs—marihuana and hashish—reported similar reactions but not as intense; there were only two or three of these reporting as intense experiences as those of users of the stronger psychedelics like LSD-25.

Reactions such as these, paralleled in a few sober citizens as old as 80, help us to understand the durability and persistence of interest in the psychedelics. Through mescaline the college freshman had achieved what no philosophy course and no art course had mediated for her, direct experience of beauty and ultimate reality that gave her life a meaning previously beyond her farthest expectations. "It permanently improved my perspective on everything," she told me, "understanding of others, sense of the beauty of life and the nonmaterialistic and similar values, but along with the here and now."

In order to understand the drawing power these drugs have for many of our youth, the reader who believes the worst of the distorted information he receives from the news media and the medical establishment has only to imagine what he would do were he convinced that the drugs would do the same thing for him as for this young woman. This is not to say that there are not dangers, except to remark that these are much less than most people think.[1] While many of the youths have used the drugs carelessly and irresponsibly, the typical member of the drug culture who has come of age knows much more about the drugs than the "expert" who teaches him and is quite capable of taking precautions against such things as bad acid, "getting busted," the wrong guide, and where *not* to seek help when on a bad trip. The foregoing basic information is essential if the reader is to find the discussion of this chapter credible. Even though he may disagree with counter-cultural assumptions, he must suspend those disagreements while he tries to see the situation through the eyes of the acid heads. An empathy with the movement is essential if it is to be understood. And it is a cultural trend that cannot be dismissed.

Literature of the Drug Culture

Among the Bibles consulted by drug enthusiasts is *Island* by Aldous Huxley, a description of his concept of a modern utopia set on an island in the South Pacific. One feature of this utopia is the use of drugs, the "Moksha medicine" that opens eyes to the mystical realities of the cosmos and the passage of life into death. Charles A. Reich's "Consciousness III" in *The Greening of America* owes something to psychedelics when he celebrates the "stoned mentality." This concept is picked up and defined more exactly in Andrew Weil's *The Natural Mind*, based on psychedelic experiences, although Weil advocates highs without drugs except as these drugs may occur in nature. Theodore Roszak in *The Making of a Counter Culture* may be somewhat more conservative, but he speaks to the turned on generation in his warnings against the worship of a dehumanized science and his advocation of those values that so often emerge from a psychedelic trip. Conversations with Don Juan, a Yaqui Indian shaman, who teaches his apprentice with the help of psychedelic herbs, are freshly and appealingly described in the books of Carlos Castaneda. Many perceptive minds, prepared by sessions with pot and trips on LSD, have been introduced with Don Juan's help to some of the great metaphysical issues. My own book, *Chemical Ecstasy*, is a scholarly attempt to inform the general reader of the religious agency of the LSD-type drugs, while I. L. Gotz's *The Psychedelic Teacher* is particularly perceptive.

Can Drugs Cause Religion?

The question posed by this heading is popularly put. As a matter of fact it is stated wrongly. Drugs cannot *cause* religion, which does not inhere in the drugs. So far as we can tell, a rat injected with LSD does not have a religious experience, which is exclusively a human susceptibility. But there is no doubt that religious experience can be *released* or *triggered* through the agency of the psychedelic drugs, including those semi-psychedelics marihuana and hashish, the cannabis-based chemicals. Among 100 users of the LSD-type drugs and twenty additional users of cannabis that I have canvassed through questionnaire and interview, there was *not a single one* who did not report at least some of the elements of profound religious experience.[2] Over three-quarters of these specifically recognized the religious element by reporting they had sensed the presence of God, a third of them to an extent never previously experienced or even imagined. Others, some of them atheists, reported

religious experiences couched in less conventional terms.[3] A
Harvard doctoral experiment executed by Walter N. Pahnke,
M. D., in which theological students were given a psychedelic
drug and attended a Good Friday service, supplied incontro-
vertible evidence that the LSD-type drugs tend to release profound religious experience.[4]

It is fashionable for self-appointed drug experts and religious
professionals to pooh-pooh such experiences as pseudo-religious
and a kind of fake. If so, one will be forced to acknowledge that
frequently the fake is better than the real thing! I have known and
followed up for ten years a 36-year-old recidivist criminal
permanently turned from crime through a psychedelic vision. I
have also known individuals whose religious experiences under
drugs have completely banished their suicidal urges, and several
atheists who have had what, for an atheist, must be an embarrass-
ing experience, for they report that they have "met God."

Doubtless the most effective way for me to persuade the reader
of the point I am making is to present two people's experiences
of an ecstatic nature, one triggered by a drug and one spontaneous, to see whether he can tell the difference. The accounts of
these people are as follows:

1. Still deep in this semi-conscious state, I was vaguely aware of the
music and the beauty of it. The Gregorian choir was singing an
inspiring chant, and I felt myself in close communication with
much of the teachings of Jesus Christ. His face appeared to me in
all of the suffering He had endured for mankind. His head was
topped with a wreath of thorns, and I suffered with Him. It seemed
I carried or tried to aid Him in carrying a huge cross for endless
miles upon a dirt road, always going away from my physical
body. I felt myself weeping. I asked many questions, and I received many answers. I felt supreme and all-knowing, yet in-
finitesimal and humble. These things are all so very hard to describe. Even as I write, I find myself reliving parts of my experience
and discoveries.

2. My "closet door" was thrown open and was permeated with so
much light that I could see clear to the ends of eternity! There was
a blinding corridor of light, at the end of which gleamed a brilliant
white city of arabesque buildings bathed in iridescence and purest
white light. I felt I saw God! Since spiritual things must be spiritually
discerned, ther are, of course, no words to describe what I saw and
knew. But my prayer had been answered many fold. Although this

enlightenment had lasted only an instant, enough light was ema-
nated to last me the rest of my life! (I have ruled out the possibility
that, being at such a low ebb, I may possibly have slipped over the
edge for a fraction of a second, and then come back—I don't know.)
But I do know I've never since been afraid of dying—it was so
exquisite and all-fulfilling.

I will now let the reader decide whether he can clearly spot the
drug experience. As a matter of fact both are typical of religious
ecstasy of a visionary kind, and both were followed by a long-
lasting qualitative difference in the lives of the subjects. Either
might have been triggered by a psychedelic drug. The second
was the account given me by a young woman of her experience
(not drug induced) in a hospital room several years earlier,
as she awaited childbirth just after receiving the news that
her husband was leaving her. The first was the account of the
criminal mentioned previously, following the administration of
psilocybin. The religious agency of drugs is not of course their
only psychoactive characteristic. Basically the experience is
nonrational (but not necessarily *irrational*) in character. Another important dimension is the esthetic one.

Utopian Communities

Throughout the ages like-minded souls influenced by utopian
thinking have gathered themselves into communities to pursue a
more ideal existence. Utopian societies, like Oneida, the Shakers,
and Brook Farm on the American scene, monasteries both
Christian and non-Christian, as well as many smaller ecstatic
societies worldwide and through the ages, are cases in point.
Many have been inconspicuous and negligible in their influence
on the wider society, but taken as a whole such communities
have been exceedingly influential as a factor in culture. Take
as an example an article in the *New York Times* that recently
came to my attention.[5] It concerns the thousands of followers of
an Indian physicist-turned-Hindu monk named Maharishi
Mahesh Yogi, who has emerged from a Hindu community to
found several Los Angeles-based societies to promote Transcendental Meditation. As an example of a new devotee there
is pictured an Executive Vice President of a Connecticut
manufacturing company, who practices meditation every morn-
ing at 6:30. He reports that it enables him to work more

efficiently, help others, and have more energy left at the end of the day for his family life. Most of the communities with such an influence have a religious or transcendental aim, mostly because profound religious experience has no equal in its astonishing capacity to activate the most durable sources of motivation within the human psyche.

Since the psychedelic drugs release religious experience, as I have demonstrated here and elsewhere,[6] then we should not be surprised that they give rise to utopian religious communities. There is of course a considerable history of utopian religious communities over the centuries, but probably the first contemporary drug inspired communities, started more or less spontaneously among the students and followers of Harvard Professors Timothy Leary and Richard Alpert in Newton, Massachusetts, in 1962. In his perceptive account of the commune movement, Robert Houriet[7] estimates that since the Newton communities over 2,000 such communities have been founded in the U.S. Most of these have had short histories and not all have featured the use of drugs. But it is fair to guess that all but a very few of the membership have been first introduced to the religious potential lying within them through drugs, mostly cannabis and LSD-type drugs. Example are the Oz community in Meadville, Pa., now defunct; High Ridge Farm in Oregon; and New Buffalo near Taos, New Mexico.

Confused and unstable though most of these communities are, their members have nonetheless become aware of the great power of nonrational religious experiences. For most of them nothing less would have caused their disillusionment with the comfortable, affluent, middle class environment in which they had been reared. Many have dropped out of school and college after contrasting what to them are musty textbooks and the boring lectures of pedantic professors *about* such abstractions as beauty, death and rebirth, transfiguration, and the transcendental, with lively face-to-face confrontations with these realities mediated through the drugs. The experience of the college freshman described in the opening paragraph of this essay is a case in point.

Utopian Aspects of Drug Related Communities

As I have pointed out, the experiences released by the psychedelic drugs are so intense that they often have profound effects on the values and on the life styles of the subjects. What are some of these effects?

First of all there is the urge to give and receive love. That a good deal of the talk about love is superficial does not mean that some of the people in these communities do not develop a remarkable sense of affection and responsibility toward one another. The talk of love tends to crystallize and to provide a salient purpose for the community. The sense of mutual responsibility is shown in the general concern for the welfare of children and the problems of other members. There are many examples of the tolerance of and concern for members who are mentally ill, for whom the community life has been therapeutic.[8]

Another interest derives from high valuation and respect for nature, intensified in drug trips. Henry David Thoreau is one of the patron saints of the commune movement, many of whose members have become disillusioned in the cities and have sought a more idyllic and simplified existence among the beauties of nature. Members of the counter culture have been early supporters of the modern ecological movement. My first sharp awareness of dangers to the ecology came from a cogently documented article on the subject published in an underground newspaper put out by one of the drug inspired communities.

The typical "acid head" usually becomes aware of metaphysical values and areas of interest that take on a greatly increased importance when he begins to absorb the lessons of his drug experience. Previously such values had been of little interest to him, and he begins to be aware of the fact that few of his straight friends have much use for those who "waste their time" probing the great issues of life and death. He becomes lonely and, like the founders of Brook Farm, begins to seek the company of those willing to "rap with him" on issues raised in Plato's dialogues or by that homespun modern pharmacological Plato, Don Juan.[9] Or perhaps he simply wishes to discuss, like many of the young people who have come to me for advice, the puzzling fact that trips on pot or acid have suddenly brought so much more meaning into his life. These concerns help to explain why many have sought the company of like-minded friends in communes or communities.

But such communities wish to express their interests practically, in some form other than in words. Since many find religious significance in their drug experiences, most of the drug inspired

communities try to express this significance in religious activities of one kind or another. Most of the communities I have
visited have set apart a room for meditation, and religious
dances, chanting, and rituals related to the rhythmic drama of
changes on the face of nature are frequent features. These and
similar activities have launched many an "acid head" on a search
for non-drug highs. Even many of those residents who have not
stayed very long have benefited from a confrontation with a
society radically different from that in which they have grown
up, and an opportunity to consider their life goals from a new
perspective.

Dystopian Aspects

One of the needs of any community is some sort of framework
or organization if individuals are to work together, no matter
how idealistic and well motivated the individuals may be. This
is the beginning of what so many utopians have rebelled against,
the institution. This means that, at least in germ, all the familiar
evil potentialities of the institution are present—rigidity, authoritarianism, bureaucracy, subordination of the welfare of the individual to that of the institution, etc. Since these evils are also, from the
point of view of the institution, virtues, it is not strange that some
communities have succumbed to them, at least in part. Houriet
felt authoritarianism to be oppressive at New Vrindaban, a
community of the Hare Krishna movement in West Virginia and
at the Brotherhood of the Spirit in Warwick and Northfield,
Massachusetts.[10] Both of these communities banned drugs, yet
included many members who would not have been there had
they not first been awakened through drugs.

Allied to institutionalism is the tendency of certain religious
communities self-righteously to insist on a dogmatic interpretation of the religious experience of the membership, rather than
to rely on the religious experiences themselves and the spirit
of compassionate understanding of others that the experiences
engender. There is a tendency of the various Jesus organizations to demonstrate this shortcoming, despite the use by Jesus
of the figure of the Samaritan, despised and hated by his con-
temporaries, to define the term neighbor. These latter groups
have often used dogmatic authoritarianism not only to keep their

members in line doctrinally but also as a means of combating sexual license and other undesired confusions. Among these confusions in many of the counter-cultural communities of all types there has tended to be a freedom with sexual practices which has led to psychological rivalries and at times to the spreading of disease which primitive practices of sanitation have only compounded.

In connection with the latter problem, the confusion as to who is to take care of the housekeeping is a prime cause for the untidiness and disrepair in which many communities are found. Theoretically the love of each member for the others will lead him to share in the housekeeping chores. In practice, unless there is a stern dictator assigning chores or a disciplined understanding of who is to do what, there is much that never gets done. This is one source of the epidemics that so often break out and contribute to the wrecking of communities.

Some communities, either through conviction or for practical legal considerations, ban the use of drugs. When there is an interest in sharing the use of psychedelic drugs, however, certain problems present themselves. When the LSD-type drugs are used there are the usual problems of bad drugs, bad trips, and "freak-outs". Usually, however, there is community knowledge about what brands of acid are good and bad, and a psychedelic community is often a considerably safer place for a "bad trip" or a "freak-out" to be cared for than is the average hospital. It is essential that the "tripper" *feel himself understood* if he is to recover his equilibrium and learn from the experience, something that is next to impossible among medical personnel who have never had the drug experience and harbor lurid concepts as to what the drugs may do to one.[11]

The laws, the police, and hostile neighbors constitute serious problems for many communes. They give rise to generalized paranoid ideas and a feeling of insecurity that weaken and poison the sense of community that ideally characterizes such fellowships. Following the finest traditions of the Inquisition and modern police states, some law enforcement agencies have been known to plant spies and even *agents provocateurs* in communities. Understandably, measures taken to guard against such persons will have negative effects on the *bona fide* memers themselves, not to mention the resulting breach between

the community and the larger society, with which it is mutually
beneficial that cordial relations should prevail.

This social breach is often cited on both sides as an excuse for
a failure of many communities to exhibit any concern for current social problems. But certainly if the psychedelics' effect is
what it is often claimed to be—an awareness of the unity of all
mankind and all of nature—then members of these mystically
oriented communities can find no excuse for centering their
attention exclusively on an enjoyment of their own inner state
of consciousness. The Catholic Church has condemned this
human weakness of many mystics as Quietism. The great
Western mystics, such as Meister Eckhart, Francis, Teresa of
Avila, and George Fox, as well as the great Eastern mystics like
Gautama, have been free of it. Yet there is no doubt but that this
dystopian escape has characterized many lesser mystics such as
some of the drug—awakened mystics of contemporary communities.

Guiding Principles for Communes

The *Alternatives Journal*[12] of December 1, 1972, features a
letter from a senior fellow at Hampshire College, who has lived
in a community and visited many others. In it he gives a list of
eight principles that he feels tend to govern the successful community: 1. A purpose consciously shared by every member. 2.
Regular group interaction in support of this purpose such as
meetings, meals, and religious services.[13] 3. A respected leader
or leaders of the community with a clear vision of its purpose
and future and the selflessness to be willing to step aside when
other leaders become available. 4. Living and working together on the same ground. 5. Drugs. Here the writer says that
widespread use of drugs is symptomatic of a community's instability, particularly in the early stages. With the evolution
of a collective aim, an organization, and a leadership, drug
regulations become increasingly important. Once this "cohesive
communalism" develops, drugs should be judged in relation
to the community's purpose. 6. There should be sufficient hous-
ing for each person to have a place where he or she can be alone.
7. Diverse ages. Though not as pressing as previous requirements,
different ages bring a fuller experience which "makes the com-

munity life seem more like an enduring process than a momentary happening." 8. The community should not grow so large as to encourage factions and deprive members of that warmth and intimacy that is one of the values of community living.

Conclusion

Utopia/dystopia with respect to the psychedelic drugs is not a theory but a living fact, as anyone wishing to observe it in its most visible form may discover for himself. But he must be willing to take the time to visit a sample of the many communities and communes dotting the landscape in this and other countries. At this point their dystopian features are likely to be most readily apparent—dirty inhabitants, broken down and makeshift dwellings, quarrels, occasional "freak-outs," confusion, chaotic diet, epidemic disease, hostile neighbors and police harassment that help build walls between the community and the larger society. It is no wonder that so many of these communities become unwelcome and psychedelic drugs get the reputation of disintegrating the individual's will and destroying the values of a responsible society. As a result inquisitorial minds fulminate on the need for "law and order" and the "softening of America's moral fiber," while insensitive judges sentence possessors of small quantities of marijuana more harshly than many a murderer.

But there is another side to the coin. There is that hopeful, utopian aspect of drug-related experience, seldom recognized by those who have never experienced the strange psychedelic consciousness, and often described as "beyond anything ever before experienced or even imagined"[14] Many of the mostly youthful pharmacological utopians speak of a reality much vaster than themselves, a reality that their parents and other "straight" members of society seem unable to comprehend. This reality fills them with awe and holds an attraction that leads them to renounce the comforts of affluence in exchange for precarious social experiments among puzzled and censorious neighbors. In the search for the substance behind the visions, most experiments founder, but some communities have evolved a well organized and viable life style, disciplined yet flexible, creative and free, usually developing far beyond the obsession with drugs that gave them their original impetus.

In one way or another some of these communities have brought their insights, their labor, and their concerns to the wider society. The most successful of them have found needs among their neighbors which they have been able to meet.[15] Individuals have achieved through drug experiences and personal interaction higher levels of understanding and compassion, commodities for the lack of which current nationalisms, social injustices and greed may overwhelm our world. Mysticism, the root of all religions according to William James,[16] is experienced in such a way as to transcend the quarreling of sects, churches, and faiths over the *interpretation* of that root. Insights into new ways of healing have stimulated theory and practice among young medical researchers associated with communities, scientists whose creativity makes the restricted thinking of the A.M.A. and most medical schools seem just this side of *rigor mortis*. Drugs have functioned as tools to reveal to many young thinkers profound new concepts of the nature of man and new ways of coping with life.

We are still historically too close to the beginnings of this movement to state definitively what the long term value of the psychedelic drugs will be or just how these potent catalysts can best be used. Prejudice and misinformation must give way to experimentation and dispassionate analysis. It will take another generation to distill the wisdom of the "acid heads," and time to demonstrate how many of their communities are fit to survive. But new juices are clearly beginning to flow and new influences have been released which deserve the serious attention of those who sense the need of new directions in national and world culture.[17]

NOTES

1. See N. I. Dishotsky et al., "LSD and Genetic Damage." *Science*, 172 (April 30, 1971), pp. 431-440, for a thorough and authoritative review of the scientific literature to date relating to the harmful side effects of LSD on humans.

2. I define religion as *the experience of the indivdual when he senses God, a Beyond or the Ultimate, especially as evidenced in his attempts to harmonize his life with that Beyond.* See Chap. 2, "What is Religion" in my *The Psychology of Religion* (New York: Macmillan, 1958) for a fuller discussion. The definition

points toward mysticism as an essential element in religious experience with
feelings of timelessness, unity, blessedness and the divine, characteristics often in
fact reported by users of psychedelics drugs, as documented in this essay.

3. W. H. Clark, "The Place of Drugs in the Religions of the Counter Culture."
Paper presented at the Annual Meeting of the Society for the Scientific Study of
Religion, October 27, 1972.

4. W. H. Clark, *Chemical Ecstasy* (New York: Sheed and Ward, 1969) pp. 77-80.

5. December 11, 1972, p. 37.

6. W. H. Clark, *op. cit.*

7. Robert Houriet, *Getting Back Together* (New York: Coward, McCann, and
Geoghegan, 1971).

8. e.g. Cave David, Dennis and Crazy Jim in the account of New Buffalo
Community, Taos, New Mexico; *Ibid.*, pp. 131-201.

9. See *A Separate Reality: Further Conversations with Don Juan* by Carlos
Castaneda. (New York: Simon and Schuster, 1971).

10. See Houriet, *op. cit.*, Chap. 8.

11. Mental Health personnel and counselors, including clergymen and some
teachers, may receive administrations of LSD at Government expense and under
impeccable supervision by applying to the Maryland Psychiatric Research Center, Box 3235, Baltimore, Md. 21228.

12. Address: Box 36604, Los Angeles, California 90036.

13. One communal group expressed to me its conviction that a meditation room
was essential to the stability of any commune.

14. See first paragraph of this essay and Clark, *Op. cit.*, pp. 81-85; 1972.

15. e.g. see statement by George Peters, Director of Naturalism, Inc., 7717 N.
Sheridan Road, Chicago, Ill. 60626, in *Alternatives News Magazine*, Communes
Directory Issue, published by Alternatives Foundation, Drawer A—Diamond
Heights Station, San Francisco 94131, 1971, pp. 3-4.

16. G. W. Allen, *William James* (New York: Viking Press, 1967) p. 425.

17. This will acknowledge help in writing this essay from the members of
Aspinwall community, Brookline, Massachusetts, where I have had a desk for
the last year and a half and have learned much.

*Siddhartha** and
A Clockwork Orange:
Two Images of Man in
Contemporary Literature and
Cinema

DORIS AND HOWARD HUNTER

OF INNUMERABLE IMAGES of man portrayed in contemporary literature and cinema, is there an authentic image which points the way to what it means to be human against the backdrop of ultra-violence and psychic isolation? So many images pass before the mind in that magic darkness of the theater or in the private world of the printed page that we become participants in the myth of the cave described by Plato ages ago. Sitting in our chained positions in the cave, we view the flickering shadows upon the screen or page and attempt to discern something "real" in the reflections. Now and then we hear voices which claim to possess a truth that transcends both the cave and its shadows. They speak about the drama of life which is discovered not in secondary abstractions but in confrontation of primary realities.

Doris L. Hunter is Assistant Professor of Humanities at Boston University College of Basic Studies and co-editor of two readers on the ethics of action, *Non-violence* and *Violence*.

Howard H. Hunter is Chairman of the Department of Religion at Tufts University and editor of *Humanities, Religion and the Arts Tomorrow*.

These artists of authenticity are similar to Plato's ideal philosophers, demanding that we unchain ourselves from the position
of seeing only pale abstractions and turn around to confront
reality without illusions.

Functions of Utopian Artists

The artists of utopian thinking assume the role of Platonic
philosophers when they seek to free man from insignificant and
often destructive levels of life while directing him toward new
levels of constructive realization. Rubem Alves in his book,
Theology of Human Hope, suggests this dimension regarding the
utopian vision when he defines utopianism as man's ability to
give names to things absent to break the power of things present.
The end of utopian thinking, he believes, is the eclipse of man's
imagination and the demise of ethical thought. Thus, utopianism
attempts to stretch the boundaries of our illusions. Often, however, utopian thought is labeled escapist, and the artists of utopia are called the perpetuators of the grand illusion of perfectibility. When utopian thought turns out to be reconstructionist
and not escapist in nature (using Lewis Mumford's terms), it is
because it has proven to be "practical" and not visionary in
quality.[1] Perhaps it is this awareness of man's deep suspicion
of any perfected utopian scheme which encourages some literary
artists to use satire to convey their hope for mankind's future. To
paint a negative picture of utopia-dystopia is to warn us
against any static and impersonal dream of perfectibility.

Two literary artists of utopia, Plato and Aldous Huxley, use
both utopian and dystopian thought to present their views of
salvation. Plato describes the destruction of his utopia, *The
Republic*, in terms of political disintegration, which is in turn a
portrayal of man's moral fraility, his finitude. *The Republic* can
only be established in the mind of the philosopher. The world
of the senses cannot sustain its truth. Huxley envisions dystopia
in the novel *Brave New World* (1932), and then in his final
years, after experiencing the reality of utopia in his own private
life, writes his utopian novel, *Island* (1962).

In both literary utopias and dystopias and in actual social
experiments such as the American communities of the Shakers,
the Hutterites or the Owenites, the search for the ideal focuses
on one question: what is the authentic nature of man? A second

question is related to the first—what image of man best conveys man's authentic nature? Finally, how can man move into the future, into hope, into utopia?

One direction to take in attempting to answer these questions is to examine the meaning of human wholeness in relationship to human hope. A classical view of the nature of man presents an image which is far from being whole. Indeed, in the beginning man was a whole creature in the Garden of Eden or during the period of the Golden Age. But, as various myths relate, after innocence comes the fall. Instead of psychic wholeness, man's nature is polarized by conflict, a conflict described by the observers of human nature in various ways. It is the struggle between spirit and flesh, between the forces of good and the forces of evil, between the empirical self and the Essential Self, between the "id" and the "superego," between instinct and repression, between the social image of the self and the self's private psyche. In terms of utopianism, such polarities may be described as contrasts between the private search for the inward-directed utopia and the social realization of an outward-directed utopia.

Two Types of Utopia

The outward-directed or external utopia is the more traditional type of utopian thinking. After all, utopia is not only unbelievable but also inconceivable without some external, social structure. External utopianism appeals to a social image of man whereby man can order his daily existence by directing his behavior into culturally accepted patterns. Plato's *Republic* with its precise definition of justice as the harmonious relationship between the individual and the state; Edward Bellamy's *Looking Backward* with its concept of the solidarity of all mankind in terms of human brotherhood; B. F. Skinner's *Walden Two* with its description of positive reinforcement and its resulting social engineering—all are illustrative of classical utopianism. The goal is finding that external, social model for producing that authentic image of man. Here the Apollonian god of enlightenment is idealized—the god of reason, reflection, respect for tradition, discipline, conformity to a social order, reliability and respectability.[2]

It is possible to take these virtues to their extreme—an absurd extreme, some would say. A number of writers have done so in such "dystopian" creations as the nightmare *1984* by George Orwell, the *We* society of the United State (Eugene Zamiatin), the hedonistic "paradise" of *Brave New World* (Aldous Huxley), and the ultra-violence of *A Clockwork Orange* by Anthony Burgess and its cinematic version produced by Stanley Kubrick. Yet even such dystopian works reveal in their despair a hope for an enlightened type of utopian social order.

The inward-directed utopia, in contrast, seeks a private realization of psychic wholeness. The journey toward authenticity is a journey into the self and not outward into some social expression. Here the Dionysian god of enthusiasm is enthroned— the God of spontaneity, emotion, intuition, instinct.[3] In the contemporary scene we see enthusiastic support for these ideals of inward-directed utopianism coming from unexpected sources. We find it in the field of psychology in such works as Norman O. Brown's *Love's Body*, R. D. Laing's *The Divided Self*; in sociology in the writings of Herbert Marcuse; in religion as a new interest in mysticism, the occult, and Eastern religions. As Theodore Roszak writes in *The Making of a Counter Culture*, it is being expressed by a zealous appreciation for a type of "superconsciousness" that overflows all logical and rational limits while dethroning educated respect for scientific "objective consciousness."[4] Further dimensions are added to this journey into the self in such works as Huxley's *Doors of Perception*, Carlos Castaneda's *The Teachings of Don Juan* and *A Separate Reality*, and Timothy Leary's *Politics of Ecstasy* and *High Priest*. In terms of literary utopias, Huxley's *Island* and Herman Hesse's *Siddhartha* illustrate this type of inward-directed utopianism.

Utopias and the Search for Wholeness

In his continual search for psychic wholeness, each person has before him two goals. The first is an image of himself which is in harmony with some social order (outward-directed utopia). The second is an image of himself which is at one with a personal private experience of the "real" self within himself (inward-directed utopia). Seldom are these goals compatible. One set of ideals always takes practical precedence over the other.

An example of this polarity is seen in two extreme images of man found in *A Clockwork Orange* and *Siddhartha*. A close examination of the polar images in these works will enable us to understand their writers' concepts of human authenticity. We may also see whether any resolution of the polarities is portrayed, or whether any resolution can be realized in view of such images of man.

Hesse's Creative Process in Siddhartha

It took almost four years for Herman Hesse to complete *Siddhartha: An Indic Poem*. The difficulty came for the author at the conclusion of the novel. Hesse could identify with the struggles of his protagonist, Siddhartha, as he moved from innocence to despair, but the resolution of struggle was difficult for Hesse to conceive and to describe. To experience the loss of innocence with Siddhartha was conceivable, for it paralleled Hesse's own personal awakening to that world beyond the child's dream. Yet nostalgia for childhood innocence always remained with Hesse (as well as with Siddhartha) and became a part of wisdom which is an essential aspect of the journey into the self. Hesse's poem, *Childhood*, reveals the depth of this nostalgia.[5]

By the age of forty-two, when he began writing *Siddhartha*, Hesse knew the anguish which was involved in moving from that first stage of childlike innocence to the second stage, realization—the realization he describes in so many of his novels and poems as the awakening to the conflict between spirit and sensuality. At this level, Hesse believes, we become aware of that tension between the hope of some external utopian answer for our human need and the despair of the inward self at the failure of any such answer's bringing a resolution of this need. Hesse describes this awareness as the striving for justice under the law and the consequent despair in the futile struggle to overcome guilt by deeds or by knowledge.[6] Or, again, it may be described as the conflict between the social expression of an external utopian answer in contrast to the private search for an inward-directed utopia. No resolution is possible between these goals, for that spontaneous emotional (Dionysian) encounter with life can never be satisfied by an intellectual (Apollonian) understanding of life.

Siddhartha's Search

Siddhartha experiences this tension between the spirit and flesh as he moves from his early years of ascetic devotion to the Buddhist Way into his middle years of sensual devotion to wealth, power and erotic love. Hesse beautifully describes the process of maturation in one of his poems.[7] Childhood innocence with its sustaining maternal (natural) principle of rebirth and permanence is lost as "the paternal spark" breaks through the "mother magic" to lead the child to manhood at the cost of extinguishing his innocence and kindling a conscience. The fragile creature man thus "dallies" between mother and father, body and spirit, as he suffers, believes, loves and hopes.

The search for hope begins for Siddhartha when he concludes, after a conversation with the historical Buddha, that he must find his *own* path to salvation. The name Siddhartha, meaning "The One Who Has Reached the Goal," was one of the variant names for the Buddha himself. Gautama was his proper name, while the title "The Buddha," meaning "The One Who Is Awake," became an appropriate appellation only after his experience of enlightenment. Hesse's literary figure, Siddhartha, may be for the author the shadow or the hidden side of the Buddha, but he is never in any sense the Buddha himself.[8] To acknowledge the Four Noble Truths and to follow the Eightfold Path for the Buddhist is not to say "I must judge for myself." It is not to say "I must choose and reject."[9] On the contrary, the Buddhist faithful are judged by the Four Noble Truths and accept without question the path to salvation which is the Eightfold Path. One suffers and pays a terrible price, the Buddha believed, to judge, to choose, to reject for the sake of the *self*. Yet Siddhartha accepts all these hardships for the sake of his own journey into the self.

It is Hesse's conviction that each person must make his own journey into the terrifying regions of the self if authenticity is to be found. And it *is* a terrifying journey, for it leads us to a confrontation with the chaos within our nature, a chaos which Hesse describes through the words of Siddhartha:

> I have had to experience so much stupidity, so many vices, so much error, so much nausea, disillusionment and sorrow, just in order to become a child again and begin anew. But it was right that

it should be so: my eyes and heart acclaim it. I had to experience despair. I had to sink to the greatest mental depths, to thoughts of suicide, in order to experience grace, to hear Om again, to sleep deeply again and to awaken refreshed again. I had to become a fool again in order to find Atman in myself. I had to sin in order to live again.[10]

The absolute necessity of experiencing this inward journey leads Siddhartha to the abyss by the edge of the river.

With a distorted countenance he stared into the water. He saw his face reflected, and spat at it; he took his arm away from the tree trunk and turned a little, so that he could fall headlong and finally go under. He bent, with closed eyes—towards death.[11]

What saved him from oblivion was a cry "OM" from the remote part of his soul. To step back from the moment of suicide, to begin again—and even to begin the first step into that inner journey—is for Siddhartha (and for Hesse) extremely difficult. It is possible only for the few.

Most people . . . are like a falling leaf that drifts and turns in air, flutters, and falls to the ground. But a few others are like stars which travel one defined path: no wind reaches them, they have within themselves their guide and path.[12]

Here is an unequivocal statement that the search for authenticity requires that subjective journey into an inward-directed utopia, but also that such a journey is only for the strongest who force their way through the "atmosphere of the bourgeois world and arrive in the cosmos; the majority resign themselves and make compromises."[13] Most people, though they are aware that they are no longer children, cling to their infantile world of dreams and impulses. They refuse to become aware of another level of realization which confronts the self with the conflict between good and evil, between the spirit and the flesh.

The journey toward authenticity—or toward another realization beyond childhood and beyond the conflict between the spirit and the flesh—continues in Hesse's thought and in Siddhartha's pilgrimage. The transcending of childhood innocence leads to the second level of individualized realization of the conflict between spirit and flesh, which in turn leads to the third and final level of higher innocence.[11] Higher innocence is not a return to childhood but a refinement of the spirit as it ascends without regret toward Spirit. Hesse's own poetry affords the best insight into this ascension of the spirit:

> In all beginnings dwells a magic force
> For guarding us and helping us to live. . . .[15]

Symbolism in Siddhartha

The ascent toward this third level of higher innocence is symbolized in the novel by Siddhartha's relationship to the river. In innocence Siddhartha is born by the river; as a young man he crosses the river leaving the life of asceticism behind him; as a middle-aged man he crosses the river once more leaving behind him a life of sensuality; by its side, Siddhartha in despair considers suicide; and finally during his last years, Siddhartha acts out his service to the world as a ferry-man on the river. At this stage of his journey into the inner self, Siddhartha envisions the river to be the flowing essence which contains the synthesis of all struggles including the conflict within himself between spirit and flesh. He now realizes the unity of all things in the world, and accepts that unity as part of himself and himself as part of the development of the world—the synthesis of totality and simultaneity.

The final resolution of Siddhartha's journey into the self is symbolized by a smile. In describing Siddhartha's face as having a beatific smile, Hesse conveys the conviction that the essential unity behind the apparent polarity of being is characterized by loving affirmation. It is the "visual manifestation of the inner achievement"[16]—an achievement which Siddhartha had seen in the smile of the Buddha and which now he realizes for himself—an achievement realized by the one who has had the courage to penetrate into his innermost Self.

The Higher Synthesis

It may be that the journey into the self is the only way to transform conflicts into a higher synthesis. Such a synthesis would consist in discerning diversity as unity and would imply that the self can surrender all its internal and external conflicts to the harmonious flow and unity of all things. In this context we can agree with Siddhartha that

> Every sin already carries grace within it, all small children are potential old men. . . . The Buddha exists in the robber and dice player; the robber exists in the Brahmin . . . Everything that exists is good—death as well as life, sin as well as holiness, wisdom as well as folly. Everything is necessary, everything needs only my agreement, my assent, my loving understanding; then all is well with me and nothing can harm me. I learned that I needed lust, that I had to strive for property and experience nausea and the depths of despair in order to learn not to resist them in order to learn to love the world, and no longer compare it with some kind of desired imaginary world, some imaginary vision of perfection.[17]

If such is indeed the pathway to the higher synthesis and toward an image of authentic man, then we can agree with Picasso's statement that art is a lie which makes us realize the truth. Here the word "utopia" may be substituted for the word "art". Utopia as "some imaginary vision of [external] perfection"[18] is a lie which makes us realize the truth. The inward journey into the innermost self is the authentic utopian journey. It begins with a free choice elected by the courageous few and ends with a loving affirmation of the world as it is— yet is this truly *the way* toward authentic utopianism? Is there no ultimate reality or validity to the utopian vision of a "better" world? Can we find no solace in the plans of outward-directed utopianism? Anthony Burgess' novel, *A Clockwork Orange*, sends us in the opposite direction from the pilgrimage of Siddhartha, presenting us with an image of man which is perhaps "real" enough to destroy the loving acceptance of all the selves taking that inward journey into unity and simultaneity.

A Clockwork Orange

The popular success of English novelist Anthony Burgess' *A Clockwork Orange* has been extended to and enlarged by Stanley Kubrick's film of the same name. Both the novel and the film possess an extraordinarily vivid immediacy: the characters are presented so sharply that one is drawn into their lives. The protagonists of novel and film and their circumstances are scarcely separable. They are merely aspects of the whole which itself is presented without explanation. Indeed, explanation seems curiously out of place in connection with both the novel and the film. It is a tribute to the effectiveness of both novelist and film maker that their work appears as a realized object justifying itself by virtue of its appearance. But tributes to artistic effectiveness do not answer the persistent question as to the appropriate critical value to be assigned their work. For, as it happens, not everyone already lives in the amoral world of *A Clockwork Orange*. There are still those who, unlike the figures of the novel and the film, are multi-dimensional and related in complex ways to a culture which partially controls and is partially controlled by them.

Burgess and Kubrick present a young man, Alex, who stands in stark contrast to the profoundly introspective Siddhartha. To be sure, Alex is not without the ability to think, at least in the sense of plotting, if not reflecting. He determines the course of his actions—he feigns illness to avoid school, chooses sex partners, selects victims of his violence, controls his gang, manipulates others to his own ends. Yet he does so with little evidence of a perspective on himself and his situation. Even though he undergoes an experimental treatment which concerns those most significant of personal dimensions—his freewill and his mind—he and those about him are presented as relatively dimensionless non-individuals. Their identity is derived from and exhausted by their functions. Alex's meaning, if he may be said to possess one, is certainly not discerned by himself nor by anyone save the chaplain, who departs from his stereotypic caricature long enough to observe, "When a man cannot choose, he ceases to be a man!"

It is easy to see all the figures of *A Clockwork Orange* as mere caricatures, targets for satire possessing about as much real human complexity as if they were mechanically stamped out like clockworks. There is no denying that the characters of Burgess' novel and Kubrick's film are lacking in what are regularly regarded as distinctive and normal human traits. Alex, about whom the story revolves, moves through his activities as though predetermined by a mindless force. Precisely those areas of activity and relationship which have traditionally been regarded as the quintessence of humanity—filial and fraternal love, sex, work, social and even religious responsibility—are shown by novelist and cinematist as being completely devoid of meaning for Alex. It is as though one were permitted to glimpse what should have been—or might have been—the wellsprings of Alex's motivation, only to discover not a well but a shallow saucer. Even the creative artists depicted in the novel and film, a writer and a painter, are presented without suggestion of association with humane tradition. The writer is portrayed as a helpless victim whose continuing activity is made possible only by the brute force of an uncomprehending, muscular young servant. The artist is seen as obsessed with sex and as prone to violent reaction as is her terrorizer. Neither writer nor artist appear any more humane, discriminating, or conscious than their brutishly dehumanized and machine-like antagonists.

Signs of Spiritual Emptiness

The most poignantly ironic sign of spiritual emptiness is the repeated use of that most humanistic and soulful musical achievement, the triumphant and affirmative tribute to human brotherhood and aspiration, Beethoven's "Ode to Joy" in his Ninth Symphony. There is no joy in this most joyless of novels and films—even as there is no pity, no sorrow, and no sensitivity. The musical evocation of rapturous awareness of truth which both underlies and transcends all human life appeals to a desensitized Alex—who cannot comprehend it—even as it simultaneously infuriates him as a reminder of the trauma with which it was associated during the period of his subjection to brain experimentation.

Curiously, it may be that the central place of the "Ode to Joy" is a sign of that quality of humanity which, more than any other, serves as a clue to man's authentic character. The "Ode" represents not merely an aesthetic achievement by Beethoven, though surely the ability to discriminate between and to achieve the sublime over the banal, the profound over the trivial, and the beautiful over the ugly, is an important characteristic of the authentic human being. Nor does it symbolize solely the sentiments expressed through the majestic

music; brotherhood and joy are attributes of humanity at its
highest, but human beings persist even in their lamentable
absence. How then, does the Beethoven passage function?
It provides a catalyst, an occasion for a residual and inarticulate
rage. It has a dreadful fascination for Alex. Alex appears to be in
possession of himself, a shrewdly manipulating individual who
has learned how to achieve his intentions. Yet it is the Beethoven
which haunts him, it is the Beethoven which threatens to undo
him, and it is, finally, the Beethoven which surrounds him in
the ultimate terrifying and unresolved moments of the novel
and film.

Alex, in his unspeakable rage at the sound of Beethoven's
great religious affirmation, offers reader and viewer a precious
clue to that attribute which gives him his distinctiveness as a
person. It is that attribute which also permits one to identify
with him and to find him even attractive and appealing. For
more of us there is nothing appealing about his strutting thug-
gery, his careless use of other human beings to his own gratification, and his manipulation of the technology of creative persons calculatedly to express his violence. There is nothing
especially appealing about his use of Beethoven as a backdrop
to his squalidly dehumanizing actions. But his inchoate
rage at the persistence of the Beethoven may be taken as
a redeeming characteristic. It is with the hearing of the Beethoven that Alex loses his cool self-control and becomes vulnerable
because he is no longer in possession of himself. This is the
only time in the novel and film when Alex is presented in a way
which allows a point of entry to himself from another. He
demonstrates despite himself the universal religious truth that in
losing one's self one has the opportunity to find oneself. For in
his loss of himself he is forced to seek another, to admit the need
for that brotherhood which Beethoven's music celebrates. He
becomes for the first and only time accessible and thus vulnerable.

It is not the Beethoven which causes this to happen. Beethoven's music is the occasion but not the cause. The cause, if we
can be bold to suggest one cause for human behavior, lies
in his authentic humanity whose distinguishing characteristic
here is not appreciation for Beethoven but, rather, rage. Alex
has not been so thoroughly environmentalized, so completely
brutalized by a technologically sophisticated but spiritually

depraved society of surfeit, injustice, manipulation, and violence that he has completely lost his capacity for agonized
responsiveness. To be sure, Alex is almost gone—Burgess and
Kubrick give little reason to build an optimistic philosophy. But
he is not yet gone completely.

In Quest of Authenticity

Without the capacity for rage and the opportunity, however
limited, for the expression of it, Alex—and every other human
being—would be lacking the first condition for identifying,
much less achieving, the attributes of authentic humanity.
Visitors to areas such as concentration camps or scenes of appal-
ling natural disasters such as famines have remarked that
final desolation—bespeaking a total loss of humanity beyond
recovery—takes the form of silence. Reduced to silence either
through manipulation or tragic natural circumstances, man
loses his identity. The prerequisite attributed in the search for
an appropriate image of authentic humanity is thus communication.

A minimal communication is, of course, the expression of
irritation indicating a sense of disturbed equilibrium. Burgess'
inspired title for his novel, *A Clockwork Orange*, points to the
insufferable conjunction of opposites which, properly, give cause
to rage. The clockwork is the epitome of mechanical technology
while the orange is organic. The virtue of the clock lies in its
being utterly finished so that of it one may predict no surprise.
It will conform entirely to the will of its maker. Deviation is
the definition of fault. The orange, on the other hand, is capable
of idiosyncratic growth; it has the possibility of surprise, of
variety. The orange is a participant in the mystery of life; it
lives and is unique. The works of a clock are or may be intended
to be perfect, but they are static, replaceable, and, in short,
dead.

The effect upon Alex of a culture which places so high a value
upon the efficient functioning of the social order is to encourage in him not only conformity but also an unconquerable
though inarticulable resistance. It is as though his authentic
humanity were his Achilles' heel in the automated society in
which he lives. As utopias, both fictional and in the form of in-

tentional communities, have been known to fail because of
human faults, so dystopias may fail because of persistent human
traits which may be seen as virtues. In Burgess' and Kubrick's
preview of a nearly-present future, society is portrayed as
dystopian—soulless, undifferentiated, anonymous—an automated scene for the acting out of allotted parts. The flaw in this
society is not that it lacks self-consistency or artistic integrity,
but that at its center there is that most predictably unpredictable
of creatures: man.

Two images of the Same Quest

In his struggle to achieve and to preserve his humanity, man
cannot help but rebel against a "perfect state." He cannot, either
in utopia or dystopia, change his nature, and his nature is to
seek his meaning. Hesse, through Siddhartha, and Burgess and
Kubrick, through Alex, are ultimately describing the same
phenomenon: the human being struggling for authenticity
among the temptations to perfection (including the ultimate
isolation of death).

The inward-directed utopianism of Hesse and the outward-
directed dystopianism of Burgess present two extremes of contemporary sensibility with regard to man and his self-image.
Siddhartha's smile and Alex's rage are but two of the masks of
everyman. It might be suggested that it takes a special grace to
smile at the folly of man's efforts toward resolving the unresolv-
able, or to rage at the destruction of freedom symbolized by a
society hell-bent to perfect the unperfectible. But Hesse, Burgess,
and Kubrick are not so easily explained. Like Georges Bernanos
and Robert Bresson in their novel and film, *Diary of a Country
Priest*, these writers appear to have discovered that one does not
"take grace" but rather one lives through it. The grace required for the achievement of human authenticity is everywhere,
and such is its power and its quality that it will not be defeated,
even by man's best efforts to achieve life's perfection and thus
death. It is in the sense of their being witnesses to the sempiter-
nal fecundity of life that both utopian and dystopian images
of man can best serve each individual seeker in his effort to
realize his own authenticity.

NOTES

1. Lewis Mumford, *The Story of Utopia* (New York: Viking Press, 1962). See pages 11-26 for a discussion of the terms "reconstructionism" and "escapism."

2. William Barrett, *Time of Need* (New York: Harper and Row, 1972) page 190.

3. *Ibid.*, page 191.

4. Theodore Roszak, *The Making of a Counter Culture* (Garden City, New York: Anchor Books, Doubleday and Co., Inc., 1968). See Chapter Seven, "The Myth of Objective Conscious."

5. See Herman Hesse, *Poems*, Selected and Translated by James Wright (New York: Farrar, Strauss, and Girous, 1970), page 39.

6. Theodore Ziolkowski, *The Novels of Herman Hesse; A Study in Theme and Structure* (Princeton, New Jersey: Princeton University Press, 1965). See Chapter Four.

7. Bernard Zeller, *Portrait of Hesse*, translated by Mark Hollebone (New York: Herder and Herder, 1971) page 156.

8. Barrett, *op. cit.*, page 205. See the discussion of Siddhartha as the shadow side of the Buddha.

9. Herman Hesse, *Siddhartha* (New York: New Directions Publishing Corporation, 1951) page 28.

10. *Ibid.*, page 78.

11. *Ibid.*, page 72.

12. *Ibid.*, page 58.

13. Ziolkowski, pages 59-60.

14. *Ibid.*, See Chapter Four, "The Triadic Rhythm of Humanization."

15. Zeller, pages 152-153.

16. Ziolkowski, page 171.

17. Hesse, *Siddhartha*, page 116.

18. *Ibid.*

BIBLIOGRAPHY

(Works marked * are available in paperbound editions.)

I. GENERAL DISCUSSIONS OF UTOPIAN THOUGHT

Boguslaw, Robert. *The New Utopians: A Study of System Design and Social Change. Englewood Cliffs, N. J.: Prentice Hall, 1965.

Buber, Martin. *Paths in Utopia, trans. R. F. C. Hull. Boston: Beacon Press, 1949.

Dubos, Rene. *The Dreams of Reason: Science and Utopias. New York: Columbia University Press, 1961.

Horsburg, H. J. N. "The Relevance of the Utopian." Ethics 67 (1957), 127-138.

Kanter, Rosabeth M. *Commitment and Community: Communes and Utopia in Sociological Perspective. Cambridge, Mass.:

————. "Commitment and Social Organization: A Study of Commitment Mechanisms in Utopian Communities." American Sociological Review 33 (Aug. 1968), 499-517.

Kessler, Martin. "Power and the Perfect State". Political Science Quarterly LXXII (1957), 565-577.

Mannheim, Karl. *Ideology and Utopia: An Introduction to the Sociology of Knowledge, trans. by Louis Wirth and Edward Shils. New York: Harcourt, Brace, 1956. Chap. IV. "The Utopian Mentality".

Manuel, Frank (ed.). *Utopias and Utopian Thought. Boston: Houghton Mifflin, 1966.

Mead, Margaret. "Toward More Vivid Utopias". Science 126 (Nov. 1957), 957-961.

Moore, Wilbert E. "The Utility of Utopias." American Sociological Review 31 (Dec. 1966), 765-772.

Morgan, Arthur E. *Nowhere Was Somewhere: How History Makes Utopias and Utopias Makes History*. Chapel Hill, N.C.: University of North Carolina Press, 1946.

Passmore, John. *The Perfectibility of Man*. New York: Scribner's, 1970.

Richter, Peyton E. (ed.). *Utopias: Social Ideals and Communal Experiments*. Boston: Holbrook Press, 1971.

Riesman, David. "Some Observations on Community Plans and Utopia" in *Selected Essays from Individualism Reconsidered*. New York: Doubleday, 1955.

Skinner, B. F. *Beyond Freedom and Dignity*. New York: Knopf, 1971.

Shklar, Judith. *After Utopia*. Princeton, N.J.: Princeton University Press, 1957.

Sibley, Mulford Q. "Apology for Utopia, II". *The Journal of Politics* II (May, 1940), 165-188.

Sommer, Robert. "Planning 'Notplace' for Nobody". *Saturday Review* 52 (April 5, 1969), 67-69.

Williams, Donald C. "The Social Scientist as Philosopher and King". *Philosophical Review* LVIII (1949), 345-359.

Wolff, Robert P. *In Defense of Anarchism*. New York: Harper and Row, 1970.

II. UTOPIAN FICTION

A. *Collections*

Johnson, J. W., ed. *Utopian Literature, a Selection*. New York: The Modern Library, 1968.

Negley, Glenn and J. M. Patrick. *The Quest for Utopia: An Anthology of Imaginary Societies*. Garden City, N. Y.: Doubleday, 1952.

Manuel, Frank. E., and Fritzie P., eds. *French Utopias: An Anthology of Ideal Societies*. New York: The Free Press, 1966.

B. *Historical Surveys*

Armytage, W. H. G. *Yesterday's Tomorrows: A Historical Survey of Future Societies*. London: Routledge & Kegan Paul, 1968.

Bernieri, Marie Louise. *Journey Through Utopia*. London: Routledge & Kegan Paul, 1950.

Hertzler, Joyce O. *The History of Utopian Thought*. New York: Macmillan Co., 1923.

Mumford, Lewis. **The Story of Utopias*. New York: The Viking Press, 1962.

Parrington, Jr., Vernon Louis. *American Dreams: A Study of American Utopias*. Providence, R.I.: Brown University Press, 1947.

C. *Critical Discussions*

Hillegas, Mark R. "Dystopian Science Fiction: New Index to the Human Situation". *New Mexico Quarterly* XXXI (1961), 238-249.

_____ . *The Future as Nightmare: H. G. Wells and the Anti-Utopians*. New York: Oxford University Press, 1967.

Wagar, W. Warren. **The City of Man: Prophecies of a World Civilization in Twentieth Century Thought*. Baltimore, Md.: Penguin Books, 1963.

_____ . *H. G. Wells and the World State*. New Haven: Yale University Press, 1961.

Walsh, Chad. *From Utopia to Nightmare*. New York: Harper and Row, 1962.

Weber, Eugen. "The Anti-Utopia of the Twentieth Century." *The South Atlantic Quarterly* LVIII (Summer, 1959), 440-447.

Woodcock, George. "Utopias in Negative." *Sewanee Review* LXIV (1956), 81-97.

D. *Recent Utopian and Dystopian Fiction*

Burgess, Anthony. **A Clockwork Orange*. New York: Ballantine, 1971.

_____ . **The Wanting Seed*. New York: Ballantine, 1970.

Heinlein, Robert A. **Stranger in a Strange Land*. New York: Putnam's, 1961.

Huxley, Aldous. **Island*. New York: Harper & Row, 1962.

Rand, Ayn. **Atlas Shrugged*. New York: Random House, 1957.

*_____ . **Anthem*. New York: New American Library, 1946.

Rimer, Robert. **The Harrad Experiment*. New York: Bantam, 1971.

Young, Michael. **The Rise of the Meritocracy, 1879-2033*. New York: Random House, 1959.

E. *Some Classics of Utopian/dystopian literature*

Plato. *The Republic.* (many editions)
More, Thomas. *Utopia.* (many editions)
Morris, William. *News from Nowhere.* London: Longmans, Green, 1934.
Bellamy, Edward, *Looking Backward.* New York: New American Library, 1960.
———. *Equality.* New York: D. Appleton, 1897.
Butler, Samuel. *Erewhon* and *Erewhon Revisted.* Baltimore, Penguin Books.
Howells, William Dean. *A Traveler from Altruria.* New York: Harpers, 1908.
Wells, H. G. *A Modern Utopia.* Lincoln, Neb.: Univ. of Nebraska Press, 1905.
———. *Men Like Gods.* North Hollywood, Calif.: Leisure Books, 1923.
Zamiatin, Eugene. *We.* New York: Dutton, 1924.
London, Jack. *The Iron Heel.* New York: Macmillan, 1908.
Huxley, Aldous. *Brave New World.* New York: Harper-Row, 1932.
Orwell, George. *1984.* New York: New American Library, 1949.
Skinner, B. F. *Walden Two.* New York: Macmillan, 1960.

F. *Studies of Science Fiction*

Amis, Kingsley: *New Maps of Hell: A Survey of Science Fiction,* New York: Harcourt Brace, 1960.
Bailey, J. O. *Pilgrims Through Space and Time: Trends and Patterns in Scientific and Utopian Fiction.* New York: Argus Books, 1947.
Baxter, John. *Science Fiction in the Cinema.* New York: Paperback Library, 1970.
Davenport, Basil, *et. al. *The Science Fiction Novel: Imagination and Social Criticism.* Chicago: Advent Publishers, 1964.
Gerber, Richard. *Utopian Fantasy: A Study of English Utopian Fiction since the End of the Nineteenth Century.* London, Routledge & Kegan Paul, 1955.
Moskowitz, Sam. *Explorers of the Infinite: Shapers of Science Fiction.* New York: Meridian, 1963.
———. *Seekers of Tomorrow: Masters of Modern Science Fiction.* New York: Balantine, 1967.

III. UTOPIAN COMMUNAL EXPERIMENTS

A. *Historical Surveys*

Armytage, W. H. G. *Heavens Below: Utopian Experiments in England, 1560-1960.* Toronto: University of Toronto Press, 1961.

Bestor, Arthur E. *Backwoods Utopias: The Sectarian and Owenite Phases of Communitarian Socialism in America: 1663-1829.* Philadelphia: University of Pennsylvania Press, 1950.

Calverton, V. F. *Where Angels Dared to Tread.* Indianapolis: Bobbs-Merrill, 1941.

Holloway, Mark, *Heavens on Earth: Utopian Communities in America, 1680-1880.* New York: Dover Publications, 1966.

Hine, William A. *American Communities and Cooperative Colonies,* 2nd rev. edition. Chicago: Charles H. Kerr and Company, 1908.

Hine, Robert V. *California's Utopian Colonies.* New Haven: Yale University Press, 1966.

Fogarty, Robert S. *American Utopianism. (Primary Sources in American History.)* Itasca, Ill., F. E. Peacock, 1972.

Nordhoff, Charles. *The Communist Societies of the United States.* New York: Schocken Books, 1965).

Noyes, John H. *History of American Socialisms.* New York: Dover Publications, 1966.

Pease, William H., and Jane. *Black Utopias: Negro Communal Experiments in America.* Madison, Wisconsin: The State Historical Society of Wisconsin, 1963.

Webber, Everett. *Escape to Utopia, the Communal Movement in America.* New York: Hastings House, 1959.

B. *Contemporary*

Atcheson, Robert. *The Bearded Lady: Going on the Commune Trip and Beyond.* New York: John Day, 1971.

Fairfield, Richard. *Communes, U.S.A.* Baltimore: Penguin Books, 1972.

Hedgepeth, William, and Dennis Stock. *The Alternative: Communal Life in the New America.* New York: Collier Books, 1970.

Houriet, Robert. *Getting Back Together.* New York: Avon, 1971.

Katz, Elia. *Armed Love. New York: Holt, 1971.

Otto, Herbert A. "Communes: The Alternative Life-Style". *Saturday Review* 54 (April 24, 1971), 16-21.

Peters, Victor. *All Things Common: The Hutterian Way of Life.* Minneapolis: University of Minnesota Press, 1965.

Roberts, Ron E. *The New Communes: Coming Together in America.* Englewood Cliffs, N.J.: Prentice-Hall, 1971.

Spiro, Melford E. *Kibbutz: Venture in Utopia.* Cambridge, Mass.: Harvard University Press, 1956.

Zablocki, Benjamin. *The Joyful Community.* Baltimore, Penguin Books, 1971.

IV. RECENT UTOPIAN PROPOSALS AND DISCUSSIONS

Cox, Harvey. *The Feast of Fools.* Cambridge, Mass.: Harvard University Press, 1969.

Fuller, R. Buckminster. *Utopia or Oblivion?* New York: Bantam, 1969.

Goodman, Paul. *Utopian Essays and Practical Proposals.* New York: Random House, 1964.

Fromm, Erich. *The Revolution of Hope.* New York: Bantam Books, 1968.

Goodman, Percival and Paul. *Communitas: Means of Livelihood and Ways of Life.* New York: Random House, 1960.

Hoffman, Abbie. *Revolution for the Hell of it.* New York: Pocket Books, 1968.

Illich, Ivan. *Deschooling Society.* New York: Harper-Row, 1972.

King, Martin Luther. *Where Do We Go From Here: Chaos or Community?* New York: Harper and Row, 1967.

Leary, Timothy. *High Priest.* New York: World, 1968.

———. *The Politics of Ecstasy.* New York: Putnam's, 1968.

Leonard, George B. *Education and Ecstasy.* New York: Delacorte Press

McCluhan, Marshall. *Understanding Media: The Extensions of Man,* New York: Signet, 1968.

Marcuse, Herbert. *An Essay on Liberation.* Boston: Beacon Press, 1969.

Neill, A. S. *Summerhill.* New York: Hart, 1964.

Reich, Charles. *The Greening of America.* New York: Random House, 1970.

Revel, Jean-Francois. *Without Marx and Jesus.* New York: Doubleday, 1971.

Roszak, Theodore. **The Making of the Counter Culture.* New York: Doubleday, 1969.

Rubin, Jerry. **Do it!* New York: Ballantine, 1970.

Yablonsky, Lewis. **Synanon: The Tunnel Back.* Baltimore: Penguin Books, 1967.

V. FUTUROLOGY—PROJECTIONS INTO THE FUTURE

A. *Non-Fictional Speculations*

Bell, Daniel, ed. *Toward the Year 2000: Work in Progress.* Boston: Houghton Mifflin, 1968. (Reprint of *Daedalus* 96, Summer, 1967)

Brown, Norman. **The Challenge of Man's Future.* New York: Viking, 1954.

Clarke, Arthur C. **Profiles of the Future.* New York: Harper-Row, 1963.

Chase, Stuart. **The Most Probable World.* New York: Harper-Row, 1968.

Darwin, Charles Galton. *The Next Million Years.* London: R. Hart-Davis, 1952.

Dunstan, Mary Jane, and Patricia W. Garland, eds. **Worlds in the Making: Probes for Students of the Future.* Englewood Cliffs, N.J.: Prentice-Hall, 1970.

Ernst, Morris. *Utopia, 1976.* New York: Rinehart & Company, 1955.

Ferkiss, Victor. **Technological Man: the Myth and the Reality.* New York: Mentor, 1969.

Finer, Herman. *The Road to Reaction.* Boston, Little Brown & Co., 1945.

Garbor, Dennis. *Inventing the Future.* New York: Knopf, 1963.

Jaspers, Karl. **The Future of Mankind.* Chicago: Univ. of Chicago Press, 1961.

Kahn, Hermann and Anthony J. Wiener. *The Year 2000: A Framework for Speculation on the Next Thirty-three Years.* New York: Macmillan, 1967.

Kostelanetz, Richard, ed. **Social Speculations: Visions for Our Time.* New York: William Morrow, 1971.

McHale, John. *The Future of the Future. New York: Ballantine, 1969.

Seindenberg, Roderick. *Post-Historic Man. Boston: Beacon Press, 1950.

Shonfield, Andrew. "Thinking About the Future". Encounter XXXII (February, 1969), 15-26.

Theobald, Robert. An Alternative Future for America. Chicago: Swallow Press, 1968.

_____ . Futures Conditional. Indianapolis: Bobbs-Merrill, 1972.

Toffler, Alvin. *Future Shock. New York: Random House, 1970.

Young, Michael, ed. Forecasting and the Social Sciences. London: Heinemann, 1968.

B. Recent Fictional Projections into the Future

Clarke, Arthur C. *Childhood's End. New York: Ballantine, 1953.

_____ . *2001: A Space Odyssey. New York: Signet, 1968.

Disch, Thomas M., ed. *The Ruins of Earth: An Anthology of Stories of the Immediate Future. New York: Berkley, 1971.

Harrison, Harry, ed. The Year 2000: An Anthology. New York: Berkeley, 1970.

Stapleton, Olaf. *Last and First Men and Star Maker; Two Science Fiction Novels. New York: Dover, 1968.

VI. CRITICISM OF UTOPIAN THOUGHT

Dahrendorf, Ralf. "Out of Utopia: Toward a Reorientation of Sociological Analysis." The American Journal of Sociology LXIV (Sept. 1958), 115-127.

Hacker, Andrew. "The Specter of Predictable Man", The Antioch Review, XIV (1954), 195-207.

_____ . The End of the American Era. New York: Atheneum.

_____ . "Dostoevsky's Disciples: Man and Sheep in Political Theory", The Journal of Politics XVII (1955), 590-613.

Hayek, Friedrich A. *The Road to Serfdom. Chicago: University of Chicago Press, 1944.

Huxley, Aldous. *Brave New World Revisited. New York: Bantam, 1968.

Kateb, George. *Utopia and its Enemies. New York: Free Press of Glencoe, 1963.

_____ . ed. *Utopia. New York: Atherton Press, 1971.

Krutch, Joseph Wood. *The Measure of Man: On Freedom, Human Values, Survival and the Modern Temper.* Indianapolis: Bobbs-Merrill, 1953.

Molnar, Thomas. *Utopia, the Perennial Heresy.* New York: Sheed & Ward, 1967.

Popper, Karl. **The Open Society and its Enemies.* Princeton, N.J.: Princeton University Press, 1950.

――――― . "Utopia and Violence", *Hibbert Journal* XLVI (1947-48), 109-116.

Rogers, Carl R., and B. F. Skinner. "Some Issues Concerning the Control of Human Behavior," *Science* CXXIV (1956), 1057-1066.

Nobile, Philip, ed. *The Con III Controversy: The Critics Look at The Greening of America.* New York: Pocket Books, 1971.

VII. SPECIAL STUDIES

Eurich, Nell. *Science and Utopia.* Cambridge, Mass.: Harvard University Press, 1967.

Elliott, Robert C. *The Shape of Utopia: Studies in a Literary Genre.* Chicago: Chicago University of Chicago Press, 1970.

Ozmon, Howard. *Utopias and Education.* Minneapolis: Burgess, 1969.

Plath, David. *Aware of Utopia.* Urbana: University of Illinois Press, 1971.

Weiss, Mirian Strauss. *A Lively Corpse.* South Brunswick, Conn. and New York: A. S. Barnes & Co., 1969. (On Religion and Utopia)

VIII. JOURNALS ON COMMUNAL EXPERIMENTS, COUNTER-CULTURE, AND UTOPIAS

Alternatives Newsmagazine.
Alternative Society.
Communitas.
Mother Earth News.
Walden Three Communitarian.

1 2 3 4 5 6 7 8 9—PP—82 81 80 79 78 77 76 75 74